Spelunking Scripture:
Easter

Exploring Important Passages of the Bible

BRUCE C. SALMON

© 2022
Published in the United States by Nurturing Faith, Macon, GA.
Nurturing Faith is a book imprint of Good Faith Media (goodfaithmedia.org).
Library of Congress Cataloging-in-Publication Data is available.

ISBN: 978-1-63528-177-4

All rights reserved. Printed in the United States of America.

All scripture citations are from the New Revised Standard Version (NRSV)
unless otherwise indicated.

Contents

Introduction v

Chapter 1: Raised from the Dead 1
    The Earth Moved (Matt. 28:1-10) 1
    The Game Changer (Matt. 28:1-10) 5
    Eucatastrophe (Matt. 28:1-10) 8

Chapter 2: They Took the Money 13
    The Story Is True (Matt. 28:11-15) 13
    Is God Dead? (Matt. 28:11-20) 16
    The Last Deception (Matt. 27:62-66, 28:12-15) 20

Chapter 3: He Is Not Here 25
    The Rest of the Story, Part 1 (Mark 15:42–16:8) 25
    The Rest of the Story, Part 2 (Mark 16:9-20) 28
    The Unfinished Story (Mark 16:9-20) 32

Chapter 4: The Empty Tomb 35
    Death Was Arrested (Luke 24:1-12) 35
    Heaven Is for Real (Luke 24:1-11) 38
    The Third Day (Luke 24:1-12) 41

Chapter 5: The Road to Emmaus 45
    The Walk to Emmaus (Luke 24:13-35) 45
    Breaking of the Bread (Luke 24:13-35) 49
    The Back Roads of Life (Luke 24:13-35) 51

Chapter 6: Jesus Appears to His Disciples 55
    What's the Least I Can Believe? (Luke 24:36-49) 55
    More Than a Cameo (Luke 24:36-49) 58
    What's Next? (Luke 24:36-49) 61

Chapter 7: The First Day 65
    The Tomb Is Empty (John 20:1-10) 65
    By Dawn's Early Light (John 20:1-10) 69
    24 Hours of Hope (John 20:1-10) 71

Chapter 8: Jesus Appears to Mary 75
    He Calls You by Name (John 20:11-18a) 75
    Surprise and Expectation (John 20:11-18a) 78
    Jesus Is Alive! (John 20:1-18, 1 Cor. 15:3b-7) 81

Chapter 9: Jesus Appears to the Disciples 85
    Fear and Doubt (John 20:19-25) 85
    Known by the Scars (John 20:19-23) 88
    Receive the Holy Spirit (John 14:15-17, 16:5-15, 20:19-23) 91

Chapter 10: Jesus Appears to Thomas 95
    Beyond Doubt (John 20:24-29) 95
    Thomas: From Doubt to Faith (John 20:19-29) 98
    Doubt and Faith (John 20:24-31) 101

Chapter 11: The Last Breakfast 105
    Breakfast with Jesus (John 21:1-14) 105
    Fish for Breakfast? (John 21:1-14) 108
    The Last Breakfast (John 21:1-14) 111

Chapter 12: Do You Love Me? Follow Me 115
    The Power of Words (John 21:15-19) 115
    The Secret to Contentment (John 21:15-17) 118
    Feed My Sheep (John 21:15-17) 121

About the Author 125

Introduction

The resurrection of Jesus is the linchpin of the Christian faith. As Paul wrote, "If Christ hasn't been raised, then your faith is worthless" (1 Cor. 15:17a CEB). Without Easter, there would be no church. All four gospels present the resurrection of Jesus as historical occurrence, and most of the other books of the New Testament allude to or elucidate the meaning of the Resurrection. In Acts 1:1-8, the risen Christ commissions the apostles and promises them the gift of the Holy Spirit. And Paul explicitly refers to the Resurrection in most of his letters.

- In Romans 1:4, Paul describes Jesus as "publicly identified as God's Son with power through his Resurrection from the dead" (CEB).
- In 1 Corinthians 15:3-4, Paul summarizes the gospel message: "that Christ died for our sins in accordance with the scriptures, and that he was buried, and that he was raised on the third day in accordance with the scriptures."
- In 2 Corinthians 1:9, Paul speaks of "God who raises the dead."
- In Galatians 1:1, Paul introduces himself as an apostle "through Jesus Christ and God the Father, who raised him from the dead."
- In Ephesians 1:20, Paul writes, "God put this power to work in Christ when he raised him from the dead."
- In Philippians 3:10, Paul declares: "I want to know Christ and the power of his resurrection."
- In Colossians 1:18, Paul describes Christ Jesus as "the firstborn from the dead."
- In 1 Thessalonians 1:9-10, Paul challenges his readers "to serve a living and true God, and to wait for his Son from heaven, whom he raised from the dead."
- In 2 Thessalonians 2:1-12, Paul's teaches about the day of the Lord and that the second coming of Christ presumes the Resurrection.
- In 2 Timothy 2:8, Paul says: "Remember Jesus Christ, raised from the dead."

And it is not just the gospel writers and Paul who talk about the resurrection of Jesus.

- Hebrews 13:20-21 provides this benediction: "Now may the God of peace, who brought back from the dead our Lord Jesus…make you complete."
- In 1 Peter 1:3 we read, "Blessed be the God and Father of our Lord Jesus Christ! By his great mercy he has given us a new birth into a living hope through the resurrection of Jesus Christ from the dead."
- In Revelation 1:5, John calls Jesus Christ "the firstborn of the dead."

So, the resurrection of Jesus is a recurrent theme in most of the books of the New Testament. That Jesus died for our sins and was raised to new life by the power of God is the heart of the gospel.

Easter is the most important day of the Christian year. Thus, it seems fitting that we should read and study the accounts on which Easter is based, namely the stories in Matthew, Mark, Luke, and John about the resurrection of Jesus from the dead.

The goal of this study is to move beneath the surface of the stories to explore what the Resurrection means for our lives. This is the method of "spelunking scripture." As we examine each passage, we move beyond the details of the narrative to probe how it speaks to us, and to seek connections with life today. Each resurrection narrative, or post-resurrection appearance, is interpreted by three sermons. The sermons are designed to bring the resurrection of Jesus into our time and circumstance, and to enable us to recognize the risen Christ in our midst.

Spelunking Scripture is a series of studies based on some of the most important passages of the Bible. Other volumes in this series include *Christmas*, *The Letters of Paul*, and *Acts and the General Epistles of the New Testament*. The *Easter* study focuses on the passages in the Gospels that tell about the Resurrection, just as the Christmas study focuses on the birth narratives. All scripture is inspired, but not every passage of scripture is of equal importance. These passages of scripture that tell the story of the resurrection of Jesus are among the most important ones in the Bible.

CHAPTER 1

RAISED FROM THE DEAD
(Matt. 28:1-10)

> *But the angel said to the women, "Don't be afraid. I know that you are looking for Jesus who was crucified. He isn't here, because he's been raised from the dead, just as he said." (Matt. 28:5-6a CEB)*

The first Easter is described in Matthew 28:1-10, Mark 16:1-8, Luke 24:1-12, and John 20:1-10. Some details are common to the Synoptic accounts of the resurrection of Jesus in Matthew, Mark, and Luke: Women came to the tomb early on Sunday morning. The body of Jesus was missing. They were met by an angelic visitation. They learned that Jesus had been raised from the dead. In John's account, the stone is rolled away and the tomb is empty and angels are there, but the focus is on the risen Jesus appearing to Mary Magdalene.

In Matthew's account, the women are identified as Mary Magdalene and the other Mary. There was a great earthquake, and an angel of the Lord, descending from heaven, came and rolled back the stone that had sealed the entrance to the tomb. Those guarding the tomb were so overcome with fear that they fainted. But the angel said to the women, "Do not be afraid; I know that you are looking for Jesus who was crucified. He is not here; for he has been raised."

Upon seeing that the tomb was empty, the women left quickly, with fear and great joy, to go tell the disciples. Suddenly, the risen Jesus appeared to them. They knelt at his feet and worshipped him. Then Jesus instructed the women not to be afraid, but to go and tell his brothers to go to Galilee and they would see him there. Earlier, in Matthew 26:32, after the Last Supper when Jesus had gone with the disciples to the Mount of Olives, he told them, "But after I am raised up, I will go ahead of you to Galilee."

We learn more details about the first Easter from the other gospel accounts, but Matthew's version gives us plenty to think about.

THE EARTH MOVED
(Matt. 28:1-10)

August 23, 2011 was a Tuesday. I had returned from lunch and was sitting at my office desk and working on the computer. Suddenly, my office chair began to move. Now, the chair was designed to move—it was on wheels, after all. But the chair was supposed to move only when I wanted it to move, when I pushed it with my feet. The problem was, I was not pushing! The chair started moving on its own, with me in it! It was a very weird feeling. I jumped up and ran out into the foyer where I was met by our church secretary, Gloria. Her chair had moved too. What was going on?

We went outside onto the church lawn. I looked up at our church building, and then I looked across the way to St. Edward's Catholic Church next door. I noticed some men standing outside who appeared to be construction workers. I wondered if perhaps they had done something to cause our chairs to move. Maybe they had been doing excavation work that shook our property. It was just a guess. We really did not know what was going on.

Eventually Gloria and I went back inside and got on our computers. It did not take long to find out that there had been an earthquake. An earthquake! I did not know we had earthquakes in the D.C. area. I tried to call my wife Linda who was working at Anne Arundel Medical Center in Annapolis. The call would not go through. Apparently, a lot of people were trying to make calls, and the networks were jammed. After a while Linda sent me a text message saying she was okay and asking if we were all right. I walked around the building to see if I could detect any damage. Everything appeared to be fine. Still, I wondered if something had happened that could not be seen.

The earthquake was all over the news that afternoon and evening, and for the next several days. Some buildings had been damaged, but thank God, there were no serious injuries or loss of life. The Washington Monument cracked at the top, with many smaller cracks down to the base. The Washington National Cathedral experienced significant damage to some of its spires and buttresses. Masonry structures do not do well in earthquakes. Because they are not flexible, they cannot give when the earth moves. There was damage to some buildings at the Naval Academy in Annapolis. The Smithsonian Castle was damaged. The tops of four spires on the Mormon Temple in Kensington, Maryland fell to the ground, along with marble from the façade. Two apartment buildings in Temple Hills, Maryland were evacuated.

The 5.8 magnitude earthquake, which started in Louisa County, Virginia, was felt in a total of 25 states, and even in some Canadian provinces. It took years for some buildings damaged by the earthquake to be repaired. It took almost three years and $15 million to repair the Washington Monument, which finally reopened in May of 2014. Repairs at the Washington National Cathedral are ongoing, with a projected total cost of at least $20 million.

As I said, it did not take long for word about the earthquake to spread. Shortly after it happened, I read about it on a web site. According to Facebook, within four minutes of when it hit, the word "earthquake" appeared in the status updates of some three million users. Twitter reported that users were sending out messages about it at the rate of 5,500 tweets per second (that was more than after the death of Osama bin Laden). An article about the earthquake appeared on the English version of Wikipedia just 12 minutes after it hit, and the quake was mentioned in two other articles even earlier than that.

Some animals at the National Zoo were spooked by the earthquake, including some who seemed to have anticipated it before the earth started shaking. In the great ape exhibit, some of the animals abandoned their food and climbed to the top of a tree-like structure just before the quake hit. A flock of flamingos rushed around and grouped together just before it struck. During the quake some of the animals vocalized and ran for cover. There probably were lots of humans vocalizing and running for cover too. The sidewalks and parks in the District were filled with workers and tourists who poured out of the buildings. An earthquake reminds all of us that ultimately, we are not in control.

It was Sunday when Mary Magdalene and the other Mary came to the tomb. Jesus had died on Friday and been buried before sundown. Saturday was the Jewish Sabbath. So, Sunday was the first chance the women had to come to the place where Jesus had been buried. Suddenly there was a great earthquake. An angel of the Lord, descending from heaven, came and rolled back the stone that had sealed the entrance to the tomb.

Most tombs in those days were essentially burial caves. They usually were manmade and dug out of the rock and sealed with a large stone. The stone could be rolled back at a later date after the flesh of the body had decayed. The bones then would be removed and placed in a box called an ossuary. Then the tomb could be used for another burial. It was somewhat akin to our mausoleums or above-ground crypts in cemeteries. The difference is that we do not remove the bones after the flesh has decayed.

On several occasions I have conducted a graveside committal service at a mausoleum in a cemetery. Rather than removing a large stone, cemetery personnel removed a metal plate or a stone panel that sealed the crypt so the casket of the one being laid to rest could be placed into the crypt. On one occasion I happened to look in the open crypt. and I saw the casket of another family member that I had helped to bury previously. It was somewhat reassuring to see that the casket was still there.

Imagine the women's shock and dismay when they looked in the tomb of Jesus and saw that his body was not there. The earthquake and the appearance of the angel were a shock to the soldiers, too, who had been guarding the tomb. They fainted and became like dead men. But the angel said to the women, "Don't be afraid. I know that you are looking for Jesus who was crucified. He is not here, for he has been raised. Come, see the place where he lay." The stone sealing the entrance to the tomb was moved aside, not so the risen Jesus could come out, but so the women could go in and see for themselves that what the angel said was true.

Matthew knew that this was a shocking story. It was shocking to the women who came to the tomb at daybreak on Sunday morning and found it empty. It was shocking to the guards who felt the earthquake and saw the angel and fell to the ground like dead men. And it is shocking to us who read this story, because we have never seen anyone rise from the dead. As far as we know, death is final, and the grave is the end; dead people do not come back to life. The resurrection of Jesus is so far outside of our human experience that it is shocking to us, just as the earthquake on August 23, 2011 was so far outside of our experience that most of us did not understand what was going on.

The earthquake on Sunday morning at the tomb of Jesus was not the only earthquake in the story. There was also an earthquake on Friday afternoon at the cross, at the very moment that Jesus died. Matthew wrote: "Then Jesus cried again with a loud voice and breathed his last. At that moment, the curtain of the temple was torn in two, from top to bottom. The earth shook, and the rocks were split. The tombs also were opened, and many bodies of the saints who had fallen asleep were raised. After his resurrection they came out of the tombs and entered the holy city and appeared to many" (27:50-53).

So, Jesus was not the only one who was raised from the dead! The saints, those people who had died in the faith and been buried before Jesus, also were raised. All this boggles our minds. It is so far beyond the realm of our own understanding and experience that we hardly know what to make of it. Ironically, the centurion, who had been keeping watch over Jesus as he died, understood. "Now when the centurion and those with him who were keeping watch over Jesus, saw the earthquake and what took place, they were terrified and said, 'Truly this man was God's Son!'" (Matt. 27:54).

Here we are two thousand years later, and we have reached the same understanding: "Truly this man was God's Son." Jesus died on the cross and was buried in the tomb, but he did not stay dead. This conviction is at the heart of our faith. As Paul wrote: "If Christ has not been raised, then our proclamation has been in vain and your faith has been in vain. But in fact, Christ has been raised from the dead, the first fruits of those who have died" (1 Cor. 15:14, 20). So, the resurrection of Jesus means not only that Jesus was raised from the dead, but also that all who place their faith in Jesus will be raised to new life with God.

The earthquake on August 23, 2011 was felt by more people than any other earthquake in U.S. history. Some people wondered what caused it. Some web sites suggested that perhaps it was due to hydraulic fracturing (or fracking) for natural gas production. Fracking has been linked to a dramatic increase in earthquakes in Oklahoma, for example. The following statistics confirm this increase:

- In 2007, Oklahoma had one earthquake.
- In 2015 there were more than 900 earthquakes in Oklahoma.
- Oklahoma has more earthquakes with a magnitude of 3 or higher than California.
- Of the 12 largest earthquakes in Oklahoma history, 10 have occurred since 2011.

These occurrences also correspond with fracking activity in Oklahoma. The outcry against fracking has been muted in the Sooner state because 20 percent of the jobs there are related to the oil and gas industry. Yet, no other place on earth has ever experienced such an increase in the rate of earthquakes in such a short time. Most scientists who study earthquakes now agree that increased seismic activity is a byproduct of fracking. By pumping vast quantities of wastewater back into the earth, the friction that normally keeps the sides of a fault clamped together is reduced. The lubrication provided by the wastewater allows the plates to slip, causing earthquakes. That is what's going on in Oklahoma. But on August 23, 2011, there was no fracking activity in Virginia. The earthquake that we felt in the D.C. area was simply "an act of God."

The act of God that raised Jesus from the dead has touched more people than any other event in history. Yet, the most important part of the story is not the earthquake or the angel or the guards fainting as dead men. The most important part of the story is the risen Jesus appearing to the astonished women who left the tomb with fear and great joy. On their way to tell the disciples, the risen Jesus met them. He told them, "Don't be afraid. Go and tell my brothers to go to Galilee; there they will see me."

Why go to Galilee? Well, that was their home. Jesus would meet the disciples when they went back home. "He is going ahead of you," the angel said. Jesus would meet them right where they lived. He would be present to them in the ordinary, everyday moments of their lives. He would be with them always. And that is the promise of Easter for us.

Not only was Jesus raised from the dead, not only will we have eternal life through our faith in him, but he is going ahead of us. Jesus will be with us where we live in the everyday moments of our lives. That is the message of Easter: Jesus is with us, now and always.

The Psalmist wrote: "God is our refuge and strength, a very present help in trouble. Therefore, we will not fear, though the earth should change, though the mountains shake in the heart of the sea" (Ps. 46:1-2).

Yes, the earth may change, the mountains may shake, but the love of God in Christ Jesus our Lord will always be with us. On Christ the solid rock I stand. All other ground is shaking sand.

THE GAME CHANGER
(Matt. 28:1-10)

When I was 22 years old and in my first year of seminary, I got sick. I ended up at Baptist Hospital in Louisville, Kentucky where I stayed for 11 days. The doctors had a hard time figuring out what was wrong with me. They said my illness was similar to hepatitis, but they could not identify exactly what the problem was. After a series of tests, they determined that my liver function was abnormal, but they really could not do anything about it. So, I was discharged from the hospital and sent back to my dorm room at the seminary.

I planned to continue my studies. I even enrolled in classes for the next semester. But I was not getting any better. So, after not being able to go to class or take care of myself, I dropped out of seminary and went to my parents' home in Texas to recuperate. It was a long recuperation process. I had little appetite, I felt lousy most of the time every day, I tired easily, and I did not feel like doing much of anything. Even reading and watching television were a strain. I discovered the hard way that when your liver is not working right, your whole body is messed up.

As the days became weeks, and the weeks became months, I wondered if I would ever get well. Not only was it a time of physical suffering, but it also was a time of emotional and even spiritual suffering. I began to wonder about God's plan for my life. I began to question if God really had called me into the ministry. I wondered if I would ever be well enough to go back to seminary—or well enough to do anything, for that matter. The doctors in Texas also were stumped as to the exact nature of my illness, and they could prescribe no treatment other than to rest and take it easy.

Eventually I did get better, but it took a long time. When I finally was able to return to seminary in the fall of 1974, some eight months after my hospitalization, I still was not feeling well. I tired easily and felt lousy many days, but I was able to go to class and I managed to do my work and continue my degree program. My friend Gary Cook told me about a small prayer room in the main administration building of the seminary that was seldom used. Sometimes between classes I would go into the prayer room, close the door, lie down on the floor, and rest.

Despite not feeling completely well, I continued my studies. During the spring of what should have been my final year at the seminary, most of my friends were preparing to graduate. I was bummed out because I still had a semester to go, since I had missed a semester due to illness. Then, an acquaintance invited me to participate in a drama at her church in Louisville.

The drama involved a series of rehearsals, then a performance on a Sunday night at the church. I did not consider myself an actor, I had no connection with her church, and I had no real reason to get involved. Nevertheless, I accepted her invitation to take a small part in the drama, "Cry Dawn in Dark Babylon." Maybe it was because my friends were graduating, and I still had a semester to go. Maybe I felt I needed some distraction to keep from feeling sorry for myself. Whatever the reason, I took the small part in the play at my friend's church, and it changed my life.

During the rehearsals and the performance and the cast party, I met a young woman named Linda. I learned she was a widow, a mother with a three-year-old daughter. I could not have foreseen it at the time, but that was a game changer for me. Had I not joined the cast of that play, almost on a whim, it is unlikely that Linda and I would have ever met. A little over a year later, after I finally graduated from seminary and was called to a church in Silver Spring, Maryland, Linda became my wife and Amy became my daughter.

A game changer: Merriam-Webster defines it as "a newly introduced element that changes an existing situation in a significant way." The first known use of the term "game changer" was in 1993. Originally, it was used in an athletic context to mean an extraordinary player or play that would change the course or the results of a game. Now the term "game changer" is used in reference to a person or an event that changes the existing situation to produce an entirely different outcome.

Jesus was a game changer. His death on the cross and his resurrection from the dead changed our existing situation in a significant way. And the strange thing is, almost no one saw it coming.

Our scripture passage picks up the story on the Sunday after Jesus was crucified. He had died an agonizing and humiliating death on the cross and was hastily buried in a borrowed tomb just before sunset on Friday, the beginning of the Jewish Sabbath. Mary Magdalene and some other women had seen him die, and they saw where his body was buried. But with the Sabbath approaching, there had not been time to properly anoint his body for burial or to engage in other rituals of mourning. So, after the Sabbath, on the first day of the week, Mary Magdalene and the other Mary went to the tomb.

Suddenly there was a great earthquake; for an angel of the Lord descended from heaven and rolled back the stone sealing the entrance to the tomb. The angel appeared in a semblance of lightning, and his clothing was white as snow. The Roman guards who had been posted at the tomb to prevent someone from trying to steal the body of Jesus were so overcome with fear that they fainted on the spot. But the angel said to the women, "Don't be afraid. I know that you are looking for Jesus who was crucified. He is not here; for he has been raised. Come, see the place where he lay. Then go quickly and tell his disciples, 'He has been raised from the dead.'"

Raised from the Dead

A game changer is a person or event that changes an existing situation in a significant way. Jesus was the game changer of history. His death on the cross offered forgiveness for our existing situation, and his resurrection from the dead changed the course of our destiny in a most significant way. Indeed, the resurrection of Jesus changes everything!

The Bible is clear that after Jesus died a painful and shameful death on the cross, God raised him to life. Had Jesus not been raised from the dead, his death would have had no meaning. He would have been just another victim who died an ignominious death. He would have been just another enemy of the state crucified among the thousands the Romans executed. Had Jesus not been raised, his small band of followers likely would have scattered, and his movement would have ended. Had Jesus not been raised, there would have been no church, no New Testament, no Christian faith, and certainly no Easter Sunday.

But the Bible is clear that Jesus was raised from the dead, and that changes everything! Death is not final, the grave is not the end, evil does not triumph over good, sin is not irrevocable, and God is determined to set things right. Jesus' death on the cross was a horrible situation, but the Resurrection was the game changer that transformed that tragedy into a triumphant new reality.

In the fourth century a preacher named John Chrysostom (c. 347–407) said this in his Easter sermon:

> Christ is risen, and death is destroyed!
> Christ is risen, and the powers of Satan are defeated!
> Christ is risen, and the angels celebrate!
> Christ is risen, and life has been set free!
> Christ is risen, and the grave has given up the dead!

Had Christ not been raised from the dead, we would have no hope—no hope in this life, and no hope for any life to come. Had Christ not been raised, we would have no hope of forgiveness, no hope of new life in this world, no hope of eternal life beyond the grave. But God raised Jesus from the dead to give us hope—hope that our sins can be forgiven, hope that our lives can be made new, hope that beyond the grave our life will continue in God's eternal presence. Because Jesus was raised from the dead, Paul could write to the Romans that "all things work together for good for those who love God" (Rom. 8:28). Paul did not claim that all things are good, for we know that there are many existing situations that are not good: Illness is not good, suffering is not good, sin is not good, evil is not good, and death is not good. But all things work together for good because God loves us and gave his Son for us.

When I got sick at age 22 and had to drop out of seminary and return to my parents' home in Texas, I could not see what good could possibly come out of that. It's hard to be hopeful when you are hurting. It's hard to see the hand of God at work when you are in the dark. But looking back now, I recognize that God was working through that difficult circumstance of my life to bring good out of it. If I had not gotten sick, it is unlikely that I would have ever met my life partner, or be called to that church in Silver Spring, or be called to the church in Bowie where I served for 33 years. And in the providence of God's grace, I believe my own illness prepared me to be a better pastor in a way that I could not have been prepared without it. Not everything that happens in life is good, but God is at work in all things for good.

On a Monday afternoon I went back to my dermatologist for an additional excision to remove some more skin from my back. The initial surgery did not take care of the problem, and the biopsy revealed that some of the cells around the margin of the first excision were atypical. So, more surgery was required to remove the atypical cells. Had the atypical cells not been excised, they could have developed into melanoma, the most deadly form of skin cancer. After the excision, the wound was sutured with some 25 stitches, which created a scar on my back. But without the wound, I could not be healed.

On the cross, Jesus was wounded for our transgressions. And by his death we are healed. But Jesus did not stay dead. On Sunday, Jesus was raised from the dead. His resurrection was the game changer that alters our existing condition in a significant way and gives us a glorious hope.

I do not know the precise circumstances of your existing condition, but I do know this: the resurrection of Jesus can be your game changer, too. The power of God that raised Jesus from the dead is available to everyone who believes in him. You can be forgiven, have new life, become a new creation, and live forever if you place your faith in the Risen Son of God who died and lives for you.

On Friday, the sin and evil of this world tried to destroy Jesus and all that is good, but on Sunday God said, "No way!" The earth shook, the angel descended, the stone was rolled back, and Jesus came forth—alive, forevermore. No way would God let Jesus stay in the grave; no way would God give up on us. The game has changed because of what Jesus did on Good Friday by dying on the cross for our sins. The game has changed because of what God did on Easter Sunday by raising Jesus from the dead. The game has changed, and life is the winner—your life, my life, our life with God. Do not be afraid. Christ is risen! He is risen, indeed.

EUCATASTROPHE
(Matt. 28:1-10)

We have had our share of catastrophes in the 21st century. Linda and I were on a vacation trip with my parents in Wisconsin on September 11, 2001. We were staying at the American Baptist Green Lake Conference Center when my father turned on the television that fateful morning. We watched with disbelief as one of the towers of the World Trade Center was burning, and the other tower was hit by a second jet turned into a flying incendiary bomb. With each aircraft carrying 24,000 gallons of jet fuel, it was a wonder the towers stood as long as they did after being hit. Within two hours, both towers had collapsed, and a third plane had smashed into the Pentagon. Almost 3,000 people lost their lives, including the 19 hijackers who had carried out the attacks. It was one of the worst catastrophes to hit any city in recent American history, along with the flooding of New Orleans in 2005.

While the catastrophe of 9/11 was sudden in its impact, the catastrophe of Hurricane Katrina was excruciatingly slow to develop. For more than a week, weather forecasters watched and warned that a disaster was coming. The storm had formed over the Bahamas and crossed southern Florida with only minimal damage before it launched out into the Gulf of Mexico and gained devastating strength.

Measuring at one time as a Category 5, Katrina was the strongest hurricane ever recorded in the Gulf. It had weakened to a Category 3 by the time it made landfall along the Louisiana and Mississippi coasts. But a Category 3 is still an awesomely powerful storm, with sustained winds of 125-plus miles per hour. And the size of the storm was unprecedented, possibly the largest hurricane of such strength to hit the United States. The storm surge caused catastrophic damage all along the coastlines of Louisiana, Mississippi, and Alabama. But the worst was yet to come, after the levees separating New Orleans from Lake Pontchartrain were breached, flooding 80 percent of the city. Hurricane Katrina caused an estimated $125 billion in property damage, and the human toll was incalculable. The storm killed more than 1,800 people.

As catastrophic as 9/11 and Hurricane Katrina were, the December 26, 2004 earthquake that caused a series of devastating tsunamis in the Indian Ocean was even worse. Walls of water up to 100 feet high inundated entire coastal communities in Indonesia, Sri Lanka, India, and Thailand and as far as the east coast of Africa. The best estimate of casualties is at least 230,000 dead. The earthquake, which exceeded 9.1 on the Richter scale, was the second largest recorded on a seismograph. With almost a quarter of a million people killed, and more than 1.7 million people left homeless or displaced, it was one of the deadliest disasters in modern history, surpassed only by the cyclone that hit Bangladesh in 1970 and drowned half a million people.

September 11, Hurricane Katrina, and the 2004 Indian Ocean tsunamis were catastrophes on a large scale, but they were dwarfed by the pandemic of the novel coronavirus and Covid-19 disease that began in 2020. The human casualties mounted into the millions, and the economic losses caused millions more to suffer extreme hardship.

The 21st century has experienced catastrophes on a large scale, yet the loss of even one life can be devastating. Witness the intensely personal devastation caused by the death of Jesus. When Jesus died on the cross, it was almost as if the world had come to an end for his friends and disciples. They were not just devastated emotionally; they were devastated spiritually. It shook their faith to the core. If Jesus really were the Son of God, what did it mean for him to die on a cross? What did his death say about God's power or God's purpose or God's love?

To his friends and disciples, the death of Jesus must have seemed like utter defeat, pointless and devastating. As the women made their way to the tomb early that Sunday morning, it must have seemed like the end of everything. Neither they nor anyone else could see anything but tragedy from what had happened. Jesus had died a horrible death, and all that he had said and done seemed for naught. It was a catastrophe on a very personal scale, but the devastation was no less severe. Jesus was dead and buried, and with him the hopes and dreams of his followers were dead and buried too.

But when the women arrived at the place where the body of Jesus had been laid, suddenly an earthquake shook the ground and an angel descended from heaven and rolled away the stone that had sealed the entrance to the tomb. The Roman guards fainted and fell to the earth, but the angel said to the women: "Do not be afraid; I know that you are looking for Jesus who was crucified. He is not here; for he has been raised from the dead." The women ran from the tomb with great fear and with great joy to tell the disciples. Suddenly, the risen Jesus himself met them, and they fell to the earth and took hold of his feet and worshipped him. Then Jesus sent them to tell the others that they, too, would see him. It was the greatest turn of events that has ever taken place.

The Oxford professor of medieval languages, J.R.R. Tolkien, was one of the best-selling authors of all time. His book, *The Hobbit*, published in 1937, has sold more than 35 million copies in 38 languages. Tolkien followed that novel with his trilogy, *The Lord of the Rings*, which has sold, according to some estimates, 150 million copies. It was Tolkien, a scholar of ancient languages, who coined a new word to describe what takes place in a story when there is a complete turn of events, a reversal from something tragic to something incredibly good.

Tolkien invented the word, "eucatastrophe," joining the Greek prefix, *eu*, meaning good, with the English word, catastrophe. Just as a eulogy is a "good word" spoken about a person at a funeral, a eucatastrophe is a remarkable turn of events that reverses a catastrophe into something unimaginably good. In reflecting upon the life of Jesus, Tolkien said, "The Birth of Christ is the eucatastrophe of Man's history. The Resurrection is the eucatastrophe of the story of the Incarnation. The story begins and ends in joy."

In a lecture Tolkien explained what he meant by that new word he had created. He said it represents the sudden happy turn in a story that pierces the reader with a joy that brings tears. The reason such joy is close to tears is that it is a "glimpse of the underlying reality or truth." For Tolkien, the supreme eucatastrophe of history was the resurrection of Jesus. Talk about a reversal! It turned out better than anyone could have imagined.

The tragedy of the Cross was transformed by the joy of the Resurrection. Now the death of Jesus began to make sense. It was not a pointless travesty of justice nor the defeat of God's purposes nor the end of everything good. It was all a part of God's plan to redeem the world. If Jesus had died on the cross and been buried in the tomb, and nothing else, that would have been the end of it. That would have been the end of Jesus and the end of the movement he had begun. But death was not the end. A eucatastrophe took place. Jesus was raised from the dead by the power of God. And the new life that God gave to Jesus, God offers to everyone who believes in him.

Does this mean that after we die and are buried in the grave we will be raised to new life? Yes! We will not be raised in a physical form as Jesus was, but we will be raised in a spiritual form to new life with God. This is the eucatastrophe of the gospel. The resurrection of Jesus is our glimpse of the underlying reality or truth. For those who believe in Jesus, death is the end of life on this earth, but death is not the end of life. Rather, death is the beginning of a new and greater life with God.

The resurrection of Jesus does not mean that our lives will suddenly become easy or problem-free. Life is still vulnerable upon this earth, and into many lives sorrow and even tragedy come. But the resurrection of Jesus means that sorrow and tragedy are not the final word. So, we do not lose heart. Even when life gets tough, we know that God's power and love will triumph over all. Whatever catastrophes may befall us, a eucatastrophe is coming. There is a reality and a truth beyond the limitations of this earth. Jesus is Lord of life, and Lord over death, and in Jesus we are more than conquerors too.

Near the end of Tolkien's book, *The Hobbit*, during the Battle of the Five Armies, the day seems lost. Hordes of goblins and wolves are about to overwhelm the dwarves, the elves, and the human forces. Bilbo Baggins, the hobbit, almost in despair looks to the West, where the sun is setting, and with it their hopes for the future. But as he looks, Bilbo gives a great cry, for he sees a sight that makes his heart leap. Dark shapes are approaching against the distant glow. "The Eagles!" Bilbo shouts, "The Eagles are coming!" Their rescue is at hand. Somehow everything will turn out alright.

When the women saw the risen Jesus, "their hearts leaped and a wild hope rose within them" (as Tolkien's good friend C.S. Lewis wrote in *The Chronicles of Narnia*). Somehow, everything would turn out alright. The birth of Jesus was the eucatastrophe of history. The resurrection of Jesus is the eucatastrophe of our destiny. The story—and our story—begins and ends in joy.

QUESTIONS FOR DISCUSSION/REFLECTION

1. In the Resurrection story, what is the meaning of the earthquake? Of the stone rolled away?
2. The angel and then the risen Jesus said, "Don't be afraid." How does the resurrection of Jesus dispel our fears?
3. Why did the risen Jesus go ahead of his disciples to Galilee?
4. What difference does the resurrection of Jesus make for your life?

CHAPTER 2

THEY TOOK THE MONEY
(Matt. 28:11-15)

> *After the priests had assembled with the elders, they devised a plan to give a large sum of money to the soldiers, telling them, "You must say, 'His disciples came by night and stole him away while we were asleep.'" So they took the money and did as they were directed. (Matt. 28:12-13, 15a NRSV)*

"They took the money." The soldiers who had been guarding the tomb of Jesus accepted a bribe from the chief priests and elders to keep quiet about Jesus rising from the dead. The soldiers were to explain the empty tomb by saying the disciples of Jesus had come by night and stolen the body while the guards were sleeping. Never mind that sleeping on the job was a serious punishable offense! The Jewish leaders vowed to protect the lying soldiers from punishment if the story ever reached the governor's ears. Apparently, the Jewish officials were willing to bribe the governor too. We are not told exactly how much money was required to bury the truth, except to say that it was a "large sum."

The lie was still being told among the Jews when Matthew wrote his gospel, decades later. So, efforts to deny the resurrection of Jesus existed from that first Easter Sunday. But they could not bury the truth. The women were already on their way to tell the disciples. And there was this incontrovertible evidence: Jesus was alive!

THE STORY IS TRUE
(Matt. 28:11-15)

A few years ago Linda and I went to see the movie, *Miracles from Heaven*. Normally we shy away from so-called "faith-based" movies. Either the production values are not good, or the belief system behind the movie is overly simplistic. But this movie is based on a true story, and some well-known actors are in the movie, namely Jennifer Garner and Queen Latifah. So, we went to see it.

To keep from "spoiling" the movie if you have not yet seen it, here is my spoiler alert: The general plot line of the movie, and the book on which the movie is based, was well publicized when the movie came out. It appeared in magazines such as *Parade* and *People* and on entertainment television shows and web sites. The movie tells the story of Annabel Beam, a 9-year-old girl with a chronic digestive disorder. Despite visits to many doctors and multiple stays in the hospital, no one was able to offer Anna (as she is called) a cure for her condition.

In the movie it is painful to watch Anna suffer. She cannot tolerate most solid foods. For a time, she is fed through a tube in her nose. Her stomach is distended and aches constantly. After a series of missed diagnoses, a specialist determines that she suffers from pseudo-obstruction motility disorder. It is a rare, incurable condition involving the nervous system. Her digestive system cannot process food properly because the nerves do not relay the message to the muscles in her intestinal tract. At one point, Anna becomes so disheartened by the pain in her stomach that she tells her mother she wants to die.

The story takes a dramatic turn in December, 2011. In an effort to distract Anna from her illness, her sister goads her into climbing a large, dead cottonwood tree in their back yard. While climbing high in the tree, a branch breaks and Anna falls 30 feet into the base of the hollowed trunk. She remains stuck inside the tree for hours, until fire department rescuers finally get her out. Rushed to the emergency room, Anna undergoes a series of tests for neurological damage. To her worried parents the ER doctor says, "Other than possibly a concussion and some superficial bumps and bruises, she doesn't appear to have been injured at all." Not only that, but in the days that follow, Anna seems to have lost any symptoms of her underlying illness. After more tests, doctors advise her parents that they can discontinue the medications Anna has been taking for years.

Anna's father, Kevin Beam, is a veterinarian. Given his medical background, he seeks a scientific explanation for Anna's remarkable recovery. He says, "I can't explain what happened to her physically while she was in that tree. All I have to go on is the radiological data and the medical records from before and after." Anna's mother can only come to the conclusion that Anna's recovery is a miracle. Anna's gastroenterologist, a specialist who treated her at the children's hospital in Boston, is Samuel Nurko. Dr. Nurko doesn't call it a miracle, but he does release Anna from his care, noting that she is "completely asymptomatic, is leading a normal life, and is not requiring any therapies."

Was it a miracle, or could it be that Anna's fall into the tree may have done something to cause her nervous system to reconnect to her digestive system? That's a theory. What cannot be disputed is that a formerly very sick girl who used to require a liquid diet and 10 medications a day is now eating pizza and McDonald's Happy Meals.

Anna's recovery probably would be no more than a medical curiosity were it not for the fact that she believes she had a spiritual encounter with God while stuck in the tree. Anna told her parents that while she was unconscious in the tree, she "went to heaven and sat in Jesus' lap." This is the part of the story that has some skeptics shaking their heads and rolling their eyes in disbelief. But it's also the part of the story that inspired Anna's mother, Christy Beam, to write a book about it, which was made into the movie.

As I was researching background information about Anna's story, I checked out various web sites on the Internet. Some of those web sites allow readers to leave comments. Many of the comments were positive, but some were extremely negative, snarky, condescending, even cruel. Most of the negative comments do not merit repeating, but the gist is that some people refuse to believe a miracle happened. They say that Anna wasn't really that sick, or that the story was simply made up to make money. Just to give you an example, here is one sarcastic comment: "Awesome! Now I am going to jump from a tree too. I better make it 40 feet; I am pretty screwed up...."

They Took the Money

Some people simply refuse to believe in miracles. Some people refuse to believe in God, or they refuse to believe that if there is a divine being, that being would ever intervene in human life for good. The characters in our scripture passage experienced the same skepticism.

Jesus had been raised from the dead, but some people refused to believe it. The soldiers guarding the tomb felt the earthquake and saw the angel. They were so shocked that they fainted as dead men. When they came to, they saw that the tomb was empty. In a panic, some of them rushed into Jerusalem to tell the chief priests what had happened.

The priests and elders concocted a scenario to explain the empty tomb. They devised a plan to give the soldiers a large sum of money. In return, the soldiers would say that Jesus' disciples had come during the night and stolen the body while the guards were sleeping. The only problem with that explanation is that the guards could be executed for sleeping while on duty. The priests and elders promised they would keep the guards out of trouble should news of the empty tomb reach the governor's ears. So, they took the money and did as they were told. And this false story was still being told among the Jews as Matthew wrote his gospel years later. Jesus didn't really rise from the dead; the disciples came during the night and stole the body. So the story goes.

I recall hearing Dave Thompson, an astrophysicist with NASA, talking about Albert Einstein during a children's story time at Village Baptist Church. Dr. Dave said that a theory about gravitational waves that Albert Einstein offered a century ago was met with great skepticism, even disbelief, at the time. But scientists have discovered evidence that validates Einstein's theory. In February of 2016, the lead investigator of the Laser Interferometer Gravitational-wave Observatory (LIGO) made a stunning announcement: "Ladies and gentlemen, we have detected gravitational waves."

Dr. Dave could explain it better, but here is what I found out about LIGO. Some 1.3 billion light years away, two black holes, each approximately 30 times the mass of our sun, merged. The merger created ripples (or wiggles, as Dave called them) in the fabric of space itself. After journeying through space at the speed of light, the ripples finally reached the LIGO detectors, with bases in Washington and Louisiana. Both detectors saw the same signal. One scientist says the finding ranks alongside Galileo's taking up a telescope and looking at the planets. Astrophysicist and author Ethan Siegel wrote this about the discovery: "The Universe is opening up to humanity in a whole new way, and we're testing for the first time the most extreme gravitational regimes that exist in all of space. It's an incredible time for science, and an amazing time for us all to be alive!"

Albert Einstein said, "There are two ways you can live. You can live as if nothing is a miracle. Or you can live as if everything is a miracle." I prefer to live as if everything is a miracle. Given how little we really understand about creation, I almost laugh at those skeptics who deny the possibility of miracles. We comprehend only a tiny fraction of the vast universe in which we live, and we can comprehend the Creator of the universe even less. But the Creator has made himself known to us in terms that we can understand. The Creator took on human flesh and lived among us. And when sinful humanity killed the Son of God on a cross, the Creator said, "Not so fast," and raised the crucified Jesus from the grave. The guards took the money and lied about what happened, but their false testimony could not hide the truth.

At the end of the movie, *Miracles From Heaven*, the real Beam family appears on the screen. There is Annabel, 13 years old, and the picture of health. There are her parents and her two sisters. They are all alive and well, and if you were to travel to Burleson, Texas where they live, you could probably meet them and talk with them. You could also travel to Boston, and if he had time, you could talk with Dr. Nurko. He treated Anna and released her from his care because she is now asymptomatic. These are living, breathing people who can tell you that the story is true.

In his first letter to the Corinthians, Paul wrote to some skeptics in the church in Corinth who were doubting the reality of the Resurrection. In 1 Corinthians 15, Paul lists some of the people that the risen Jesus had appeared to, including Peter and the other disciples, and more than 500 people, most of whom were still alive at the time of Paul's writing. Paul was saying, "If you don't believe Jesus was raised from the dead, you can ask them." Last of all, Paul said, "he appeared also to me" (1 Cor. 15:8). Now, Paul did not see the risen Jesus right after the Resurrection as the others did. It was years later, when Paul was on the road to Damascus, intending to arrest Christians there, that he was struck blind by a light from heaven and heard the voice of Jesus himself (Acts 9:3-6, 1 Cor. 9:1, Gal. 1:16). It sounds about as improbable as a 9-year old girl falling into a hollow tree and saying later that Jesus spoke to her as she lay unconscious.

The soldiers took the money, and they made up a story to try to conceal the truth. But they could not hide the fact that the tomb was empty. And those who believed in Jesus, whose hearts were full, told the world that Jesus is alive.

So, here we are, still celebrating the Resurrection. Every time we take the bread and the cup in communion, we remember not only that Jesus died on the cross for our sins, but also that he rose from the grave to give us new life. As the old hymn says, "We serve a risen Savior! He's in the world today! … You ask me how I know he lives. He lives within my heart."

IS GOD DEAD?
(Matt. 28:11-20)

When I was pastor of Village Baptist Church, Ray gave me an old magazine. That may not sound newsworthy, but this particular issue of the old magazine has become a classic. Ray bought it from a rare book dealer and thought I should have it. It is a famous issue of *Time*. Even if you are not old enough to remember it, you may have heard of it. It created quite a stir back in April of 1966. The cover had a black background with these words in red: "Is God Dead?"

When I looked through the magazine, it was like opening a time capsule (pun intended). It reminded me of the way life was back in 1966. The first thing I did was look at the price on the cover: 40 cents. The next thing I did was look at all the ads.

There were lots of ads for airlines: Air France, Olympic Airways, Air India, BOAC, SAS, American Airlines, Braniff International, Pan American World Airways, United Airlines, KLM Royal Dutch Airlines, Sabena Belgium World Airlines. (The air travel industry was a lot different in 1966 than it is today.) There also were some ads for cigarettes, and lots of ads for various alcoholic beverages: vermouth, Irish whisky, cognac, Bavarian beer, rum, scotch, Kentucky bourbon, port, sherry, liqueur, brandy. There were ads for English Leather cologne, Supp-hose socks for men, Hathaway shirts, and Dacron polyester ties. The ads were a clue as to who read *Time* magazine in 1966. Most of the ads seemed targeted at men. There were ads for banks, insurance companies, brokerage houses, Chris-Craft boats, Acushnet golf balls, and Wilson Staff x-31 irons (golf clubs). There were ads for Fischer and Magnavox stereos, which could appeal to men or women, and one ad for Electra Sol automatic dishwasher detergent, definitely directed at women in 1966.

After looking at the ads, I looked at the photographs in the magazine. There was a photo of baseball pitchers Sandy Koufax and Don Drysdale at Dodger Stadium and one of heavyweight boxer Cassius Clay (before he became Muhammad Ali). There were some political photographs: LBJ with Indian Prime Minister Indira Gandhi, and a photo of Soviet leader Leonid Brezhnev. There was a review for the movie, *Born Free*, about Elsa the lioness in Kenya. The bestselling books back then were *The Source* by James Michener and *In Cold Blood* by Truman Capote.

A lot was going on in our culture in 1966: The Vietnam War was escalating, the Civil Rights Movement was making progress, racial desegregation was beginning to take place, the Cold War and the nuclear arms race were heating up, the space race was going full tilt, and the women's liberation movement was gaining momentum. Great shifts in attitudes and cultural mores were underway, and this extended even into religion. The Second Vatican Council had begun to revolutionize the Roman Catholic Church, and many Protestant theologians were questioning religious traditions, including raising questions about the nature of God, and even about the existence of God.

It was the 19th-century German philosopher, Friedrich Nietzsche, who popularized the phrase, "God is dead." Nietzsche did not mean that God is literally dead, but rather that God is dead as a focus of many people's lives. Nietzsche himself lived a pretty miserable life. His father, a Lutheran pastor, died when Nietzsche was only 5 years old, and the family went to live with relatives. It was only after his grandmother left a modest inheritance that the family had any sort of financial stability.

As a young man, Nietzsche was thwarted in love, and he suffered from various physical ailments most of his adult life, including blinding migraine headaches and violent stomach attacks. He eventually developed a severe mental illness and was admitted to an insane asylum. He died in 1900 at the age of 56, but his books continued to exert a strong influence long after his death. It is not just a curiosity that when Nietzsche wrote the words, "God is dead," he put them in the mouth of a madman.

Just as the rise of science in the latter part of the 19th century caused many people to move beyond outdated religious notions of the past, so in the middle of the 20th century some theologians challenged various religious beliefs. A small group of radical Christian theologians—including Paul van Buren, William Hamilton, and Thomas J.J. Altizer— became leaders in what was called the "Death of God" movement in the 1960s. They created quite a bit of controversy, reflected on the cover of *Time* in April 1966.

I re-read the cover story of that issue of *Time*. It included these words: "a small band of radical theologians has seriously argued that the churches must accept the fact of God's death and get along without him." One of those theologians, a professor named William Hamilton, taught at the Colgate Rochester Divinity School, a seminary affiliated with the American Baptist Churches USA. While it may sound shocking that a Baptist seminary professor would be part of such a movement, consider that the Christian faith has always had its share of skeptics.

The gospel writer Matthew tells us that even when the resurrected Jesus presented himself to the disciples, some of them doubted (28:17). That was a theme in most of the Resurrection stories in the Bible—there was a measure of doubt, or at least disbelief. Thomas was not the only disciple who doubted that Jesus had been raised from the dead; they all had trouble believing it at first.

Matthew also writes about a plot hatched by the chief priests and elders to try to cover up the Resurrection. The religious leaders devised a plan to give a large amount of money to the soldiers who had been guarding the tomb where Jesus had been buried. Matthew says that the soldiers fainted and fell to the earth when there was a mighty earthquake, accompanied by an angel descending from heaven and rolling away the stone that had been blocking the entrance to the tomb. At some point the soldiers regained consciousness and found the tomb empty. They went into the city and reported to the chief priests what had happened.

The religious leaders could ill afford to have people believe that Jesus was alive again, so they concocted a lie to deny the Resurrection. They bribed the guards to explain the empty tomb in this way: "we fell asleep, and his disciples came and stole the body." The only problem was that a soldier could get into a lot of trouble for falling asleep while on guard duty. So, the chief priests and elders proposed to bribe the governor, if necessary, to keep the soldiers out of trouble. The guards took the money and did as they were told. And the story is being told to this day.

The chief priests and the elders did not claim that God was dead, but they certainly wanted to spread the news that Jesus was dead. Of course, it was not a hard sell—everyone knew that Jesus was dead. His death on the cross had been a public spectacle for all to see. Of course, Jesus was dead! But then there was this tiny problem, this thorny matter of the earthquake and the angel and the empty tomb. The chief priests and the elders and the soldiers would have the world believe that Jesus was dead and stayed dead, but the Bible offers a different explanation for the empty tomb. According to scripture, the tomb was empty because Jesus was raised to life. Jesus died a real death. (Perhaps in that sense "God" did die.) The Word become flesh, the image of God in human form, did die. But Jesus, the incarnation of God, did not stay dead. And no amount of money to pay off the guards or even bribe the governor could deny the truth of the Resurrection for long.

I mentioned earlier that there is an element of doubt or disbelief in most of the Resurrection stories in the Bible. We read in Matthew 28:16-17 that "Now the eleven disciples went to Galilee, to the mountain to which Jesus had directed them. When they saw him, they worshipped him, but some doubted." Even in the presence of the risen Christ, some doubted! Could it be that there will always be a measure of doubt in religious faith?

My good friend Don Harris was a graduate of Colgate Rochester Divinity School where "death of God" theologian William Hamilton taught. I asked Don if Hamilton was one of his professors when he was a student there. Sure enough, Don knew William Hamilton very well. Don graduated from Colgate Rochester in 1962 (before all the death-of-God controversy), and he never heard Professor Hamilton speak of it when he was a student in his classes. But Don remembered that as a second-year seminarian, during an orientation for new students, he and Professor Hamilton were on a panel to discuss the relevance of the church. Don and a church history professor said that the church was still relevant, while Professor Hamilton and another student contended that the church was irrelevant to modern times.

After Don graduated from Colgate Rochester, he was called to a church outside of Cleveland. But in 1967, the year after the *Time* magazine article, Don moved back to the Rochester area to become pastor of a suburban church there. Shortly after Don moved back to Rochester, Professor Hamilton resigned from the divinity school to become a professor of philosophy at a college somewhere. Upon learning of his resignation from the divinity school, Don ran into Professor Hamilton and remarked that the trustees of the seminary probably were relieved to see him move on. Sometime later Don was talking with an administrator at the divinity school about Professor Hamilton's theological drift into the death-of-God group. The placement director shook his head and explained it this way: "Bill Hamilton left the church, and he lost his faith."

All over Western Europe magnificent cathedrals are largely empty, except for tourists. Despite a Christian heritage of two thousand years, many Western Europeans say they no longer believe in God, or that God is irrelevant to their lives. Empty churches, and a loss of faith—is there a connection?

During the religious controversies of the 1960s, evangelist Billy Graham was asked about the death of God. Graham replied, "I know that God exists because of my personal experience." In the end, that is the only way anyone can know that God exists. There is no way to prove personal experience. There is no way to prove that God exists, but we can know that God is real through our personal experience. And one of the places where we are most likely to experience God personally is in the community of faith, in the fellowship of other believers, in the church. One of the reasons we gather in church buildings is to support each other and encourage each other in our own Christian journeys. Our faith is bolstered and strengthened by our association with other Christians. Jesus is alive in the church because the church is the body of Christ, the presence of Christ in the world. Jesus said when even two or three believers gather in his name, he is in our midst (Matt. 18:20).

When the women came to the tomb early on Sunday morning, they found it empty. The chief priests and the elders would have us believe that the tomb was empty because the disciples came during the night and stole Jesus' body. But that was a lie: the tomb was empty because Jesus was raised from the dead. And Jesus is still alive even now. He told his followers, "I am with you always" (Matt. 28:20). If Jesus lives, then God is not dead.

THE LAST DECEPTION
(Matt. 27:62-66, 28:12-15)

The movie, *The Full Monty*, is about six laid-off steelworkers in the city of Sheffield, in northern England. One character, a former foreman, cannot bring himself to tell even his own wife that he has been out of work for six months. Every morning she packs him a lunch, and every night he comes home and tells her what went on that day at the mill. The deception is killing him. He laments to a friend, "She's out on High Street right now, with her Mastercard." The shame he feels from being out of work, and the fear that he may never find another job, have made his life a lie. He knows he can't go on like this, but he doesn't know what else to do. It's bad enough that he can't admit it to his wife; it's even worse that he can't admit it to himself.

It's bad enough to deceive other people; it's even worse to deceive ourselves. The theme for this scripture passage is deception. Jesus had died on the cross; there was no deception about that. Everyone knew he was dead—the Romans, the Jewish authorities, the women who had stayed with him to the very end, his disciples who had run away. They all knew Jesus was dead and buried. But the Jewish authorities feared that his disciples would try something to deceive the people. They feared that his disciples would break into the tomb and steal the body and claim that Jesus was raised from the dead.

To prevent the possibility of such a deception, the Jewish leaders went to the Roman governor, Pontius Pilate, and asked him to provide a guard of soldiers to secure the tomb where Jesus was laid. That would do two things. First, it would provide a physical deterrence to would-be grave robbers: No one would dare to challenge Roman soldiers. Second, it would provide a legal deterrence. Not only would there be guards, but the tomb also would be secured with the official seal of the Roman governor.

The sealing of the tomb was kind of like sealing a letter with wax and stamping the official Roman governor's emblem in the wax. This would have been on a much larger scale, with the tomb sealed with soft malleable clay, and the governor's imperial imprint pressed into the clay. To break the seal would be a crime, an illegal act subject to punishment by the Roman government. Pilate granted their request. The tomb would be sealed, and soldiers would be posted to guard the tomb for three days.

Early on Sunday morning the Roman guards were stationed at their post outside the tomb. Suddenly there was an earthquake and an angel of the Lord descended from heaven and rolled away the stone from the entrance to the tomb. The guards were so filled with fear that they shook and became like dead men. Presumably, they fainted and fell to the ground. When they came to and saw that the tomb was empty, some of the guards went into Jerusalem and told the chief priests what had happened. It might seem odd that the Roman soldiers would report to the Jewish authorities, but Pilate had placed them under the chief priests' command, if only for the three days that they were to guard the tomb.

The chief priests and elders assembled quickly to devise a plan. They would offer the Roman soldiers a bribe to concoct a false story to explain away what had happened. The Jewish leaders told the Roman soldiers, "This is what you should say: his disciples came by night and stole away the body while you were asleep." The guards were in a tough spot. To say that they had fallen asleep while on duty would be to admit a serious breach of military conduct. But who would believe them if they told what really happened?

To convince the soldiers to accept the bribe and join the conspiracy, the Jewish leaders offered a further inducement. If news of the story should reach the governor, they would take care of him, presumably by offering him a bribe. (According to secular historians, Pilate was known to accept bribes, if the price were right). So, the deal was done. The Roman guards accepted the money and did as they were told. They said they had fallen asleep during the night, and the disciples had stolen the body out of the tomb. And for many years after that, this story was circulated among the Jews to explain away the empty tomb. In fact, one of the early Christian writers, Justin Martyr, wrote in the middle of the second century that such stories were still being spread in an effort to discredit the Resurrection.

The interesting thing about this whole episode is that no one claimed that the body of Jesus was still in the grave. Everyone—both Jesus' friends and his enemies—agreed that the tomb was empty. The Jewish leaders claimed that the body had been stolen; the Christians claimed that Jesus had been raised; the Romans went along with the deception of the Jews; but no one claimed that the body was still buried. The Jews, the Christians, and the Romans alike all believed that the tomb in which Jesus had been buried was now empty. They simply had different stories to explain how that came to be. How ironic that the excuse the Jews gave was what they had sought to prevent by requesting the guard in the first place.

The worst lies are the ones we tell ourselves. The Jewish leaders knew that the disciples had not stolen the body. They knew about the earthquake and the angel rolling away the stone, because the Roman guards had told them. They knew what really happened; still, they would not believe. It was bad enough to bribe the guards to deliberately deceive the people, but they were mostly deceiving themselves. They had a first-hand, eyewitness report that something miraculous had happened; still, they would not believe.

The worst lies are the ones we tell ourselves because not only do we hurt other people with our deception, but ultimately the ones we hurt the most are ourselves. The tragic story of Madalyn Murray O'Hair came to a predictably tragic end with the discovery of three bodies buried on a remote ranch in Texas. O'Hair was the founder of the American Atheists organization and the leading spokesperson for American atheism until her mysterious disappearance in 1995. She was one of the litigants in the 1963 case that led the U.S. Supreme Court to ban state-sponsored prayer in public schools. She continued to agitate to remove all references to God from public life. She even wanted the motto "In God We Trust" removed from our coins and currency.

Because of her hostility toward God and religion, *Life* magazine dubbed O'Hair "the most hated woman in America." Ironically, one of her sons, William Murray, announced his conversion to Christianity on Mother's Day in 1980 and became an outspoken evangelist for the Christian faith. But William Murray never could convert his mother or his brother or his own daughter who were under O'Hair's influence.

In 1995 O'Hair and her other son and granddaughter disappeared, along with half a million dollars in American Atheist funds. One private investigator thought they had absconded with the money and fled to New Zealand. Others suspected foul play. Eventually an ex-con who had worked for O'Hair at the American Atheists headquarters came under suspicion. Police concluded that he and some accomplices had kidnapped the O'Hairs, forced them to withdraw the money, then murdered them. In January of 2001 he led police to the three bodies buried in shallow graves.

Madalyn Murray O'Hair devoted her life trying to deceive the American people into believing there is no God. But the person she deceived most was herself. Even her own son could not convince her of the truth. When you throw out belief in God and surround yourself with people who don't believe in God, that is what can happen.

Can you imagine what the world would be like had Jesus not been raised from the dead? For one thing, there would be no church. After Jesus died on the cross, the disciples were a dejected and disheartened lot. Even if one of them had come up with the idea to steal the body from the tomb, what would have been the point? They knew that Jesus was dead. Their dreams were dashed; their hopes were crushed. As far as they knew, the whole "Jesus thing" was over. No, it was not some deception that transformed the devastated and defeated disciples into men and women on fire for God. Only the risen Jesus himself could affect such a change.

In addition to there being no church, if Jesus had not been raised from the dead, there would be no hope of life eternal. Without the resurrection of Jesus, we would have no reason to believe there is anything beyond the grave. If the empty tomb were a fraud, we would have no hope of heaven. As Paul wrote in 1 Corinthians 15:17, "If Christ has not been raised, your faith is futile, and you are still in your sins." But the Resurrection was not a fraud, the empty tomb was not a deception, and our faith is not futile, because Jesus really was raised to new life by the power of God. That is what changed the disciples, created the church, and gives us hope of everlasting life. The tomb was empty, not because the disciples stole the body, but because Jesus was raised from the dead.

In Acts 12 we read that the disciples began to pay a terrible price for their faith in Christ. James, the brothers of John, a member of the inner circle of disciples closest to Jesus, was the first of the original 12 disciples to be martyred. He was killed by the sword, presumably beheaded, under orders of King Herod Agrippa, the grandson of Herod the Great. Another of the inner circle of disciples, Peter, was arrested and imprisoned by King Herod, and many other Christians also were persecuted. In fact, according to early church traditions, all the original disciples, with the exception of Judas, and the possible exception of John, died martyrs' deaths. A strong early church tradition says that Peter was crucified, upside down, probably under orders from the Roman Emperor Nero. And there are traditions that describe the martyrdom of the other disciples too. Would those disciples have died for a lie? If the resurrection of Jesus were a fraud, if his followers had stolen the body, if it were all one big deception, would they have died for that?

The disciples were willing to die for their faith because they knew the truth: Jesus really was raised from the dead, and all who believe in him will be raised too.

QUESTIONS FOR DISCUSSION/REFLECTION

1. Did the guards at the tomb of Jesus understand what had happened to him?
2. Because we have not seen Jesus, how can we believe he was raised from the dead?
3. What can you say to those who deny that Jesus was raised from death?
4. In what sense is doubt healthy?
5. In what sense is faith necessary for our lives?

CHAPTER 3

HE IS NOT HERE
(Mark 16:1-8)

> *But the angel said, "Do not be so surprised. You are looking for Jesus, the Nazarene, who was crucified. He isn't here! He has been raised from the dead." The women fled from the tomb, trembling and bewildered, saying nothing to anyone because they were too frightened to talk. (Mark 16:6a, 8 NLT)*

The most reliable early manuscripts of Mark's Gospel end with verse 8. But the story cannot end there! For one thing, we know from the other gospels that the women did go and tell the disciples that Jesus had been raised from the dead. Also, other early manuscripts of Mark have different endings, including the shorter ending and the longer ending that are appended to chapter 16 in most translations.

Both the shorter ending, after verse 8, and the longer ending, beginning with verse 9, complete the story in a more satisfying fashion than the women "saying nothing to anyone." Why the earliest manuscript of Mark ended with verse 8 is subject to conjecture. Was the original ending to Mark lost? It is evident that verses 9-20 were added later, because these verses are so different in vocabulary and style from the rest of Mark's Gospel. It is unlikely that Mark intended to end his gospel with verse 8. The angel's message "to tell his disciples and Peter that he is going ahead of you to Galilee" suggests upcoming encounters with the risen Jesus, such as those included in the other gospels.

The added shorter ending and the added longer ending in other manuscripts seem to indicate that various attempts were made to provide a suitable conclusion for Mark's Gospel. Some scholars suggest that the longer ending may have been composed early in the second century and added to Mark by the middle of the second century. Even if Mark intended to end his gospel with verse 8, the message is still clear: Jesus has been raised from the dead!

THE REST OF THE STORY, PART 1
(Mark 15:42-16:8)

He married into money, and his wife never let him forget it. As they were inspecting their new home for the first time his wife said, "If it were not for my money, we would not be here." Going into the living room she said, "If it were not for my money, this furniture would not be here." When they got to the kitchen she said, "If it were not for my money, these appliances would not be here." Stepping out into the backyard she said, "If it were not for my money, this swimming pool would not be here." Finally, the husband had had enough. He spoke up and said, "Frankly, Honey, if it were not for your money, I would not be here!"

If it were not for the Resurrection, we would not be here. There would be no church, no Christian faith, and nothing to celebrate. But we are here because Jesus was raised, and that changes everything.

When I was in college, I first heard Paul Harvey on the radio. He would begin every broadcast of his daily syndicated program, *News and Comment*, with the familiar greeting: "Hello, Americans. This is Paul Harvey. Stand by for news!" I started listening to Paul Harvey because I enjoyed his clipped manner of speaking and his captivating way of telling a story. I liked his positive, upbeat attitude and the way he ended every broadcast with his signature closing, "Good-day!" But what I liked most about his program was a feature called "The Rest of the Story." He would seize upon an obscure or little-known fact about some historical figure and tell a previously untold story about how that person became famous. Often, there was a surprise or a twist at the end of the story that kept me guessing who it was until the identity of the historical figure was revealed. I was not alone in my enthusiasm for "The Rest of the Story." For many years Paul Harvey was one of the most popular radio commentators, with millions of listeners in the U.S. and worldwide.

Taking a page from Paul Harvey, I titled this section "The Rest of the Story" because there was a surprise or a twist at the end of this story that revealed the identity of the most important historical figure who ever lived: Jesus. Yet, because we know how the story ends, because we know the rest of the story, the Resurrection is not particularly surprising to us. We know that Jesus did not stay dead. We know that the cross was not the end. We know that the grave was not final. We know that evil did not triumph after all. But to those who were there, who witnessed the Crucifixion, who saw Jesus die a horrible death, the Resurrection was a complete surprise. They were not expecting this ending to the story. That may explain the reaction of the women at the tomb. They had seen Jesus on the cross. They had been there when he took his last breath. They had watched as his body was taken down from the cross and wrapped in a linen shroud. They had followed to the tomb and seen his corpse laid in the grave. They had watched as a heavy stone was rolled in front of the tomb to block the entrance. There was no doubt in their minds that Jesus was dead.

Early on Sunday morning the women returned to the tomb with the intention of anointing his dead body with spices. Because Jesus had died late on Friday afternoon, there was not time to give him a proper burial before sundown and the onset of the Sabbath. Jewish law required that even the body of an executed criminal should be removed from the cross before the Sabbath so as not to profane the Holy Day. As far as the Romans were concerned, the body of Jesus could remain on the cross indefinitely until it was picked clean by vultures or ripped apart by wild dogs. Such a crass indignity would only add to the humiliation of crucifixion and heighten its deterrent effect against future crimes against the state. But Jewish law came into conflict with Roman practice. To the Jews, it would be an abomination to leave a body hanging on the cross over the Sabbath. So, Joseph of Arimathea, a leading member of the Jewish council, went to the

Roman governor Pontius Pilate and asked for permission to take custody of Jesus' body. That was how Jesus came to be buried in a new tomb after he died, instead of being buried in an unmarked common grave as was likely for all other convicted criminals.

Because Jesus died about three in the afternoon and there were only a few hours left before sunset and the beginning of the Sabbath, Joseph only had time to buy a linen cloth, wrap the body in it, and hurriedly place it in the tomb. The women saw all of this, and they felt the least they could do was to give Jesus a proper burial once the Sabbath had passed. Giving him a proper burial meant anointing his body with spices to cover the odor of decay. But they had not thought the situation completely through. They had the spices early that Sunday morning, but they had not thought how they were going to remove the heavy stone to gain access to the body. All the way to the tomb in the half-light of the early dawn, they discussed among themselves what to do about the stone.

So, it is clear that no one expected Jesus to be alive—not Pilate, who verified with the centurion that Jesus was indeed dead; not Joseph of Arimathea, who bought a burial shroud and provided a new tomb for a grave and rolled a stone in front of the door to block the entrance; not the women, who bought spices and came to the tomb early on Sunday morning intending to anoint the body. No one expected Jesus to rise from the dead. That was the surprise, the twist, the amazing rest of the story that revealed who Jesus really was.

We know that Jesus did not stay dead. We know that he burst the bonds of death and was raised to new life by the power of God. We know that the tomb was empty because Jesus was alive. But what does that amazing, good news really mean for us? What difference does it make for our lives? Well, the resurrection of Jesus from the dead makes all the difference in the world.

In the first place, it makes a difference in how we look at death. It changes our whole perspective about the inevitable end of life on this earth. As I was writing this piece, I received word that my friend Jim's father had died. Even though Jim and I served churches in different states, we kept in touch. His wife sent me an email on Saturday night with the sad news. I did not see the email until I went into the office on Monday morning. I called Jim at his mother's house in Georgia to express my sympathy and to let him know that his family was in my prayers.

Jim's father's death had come as a shock. His family members were not expecting it, but they were doing okay. They were doing okay because his father was a man of faith. He was active in his church, devoted to his family, a faithful and dedicated Christian who had lived an exemplary Christian life. So, while his death was a great shock and a terrible loss, it was not an occasion for despair. Jim and his mom and the rest of the family were comforted and sustained by their Christian hope. Because Jesus was raised from the dead, they knew that for those who die in the Lord, death is not the end. They knew that Jim's dad was now alive in heaven with God because Jesus burst the bonds of death and all who believe in Jesus will rise from death. So, the fact that Jesus was raised from the dead changes the way we look at death.

If you remember your geography, you may recall that the southernmost point on the continent of Africa is called the Cape of Good Hope. But it was not always called that. For centuries, Europeans did not know what was beyond the tip of Africa. Fierce storms often would buffet the region, and no ship dared to round that point for fear it would be lost. So, for a long time that area was known as the "Cape of Storms." But then a Portuguese explorer named Vasco da Gama had the courage to sail around the tip of Africa in the 16th century. Da Gama braved the raging storms and found that beyond the cape was a great calm sea, and beyond the sea were the shores of India. So, after da Gama sailed from Europe to India around the tip of Africa, the name of the cape was changed from the Cape of Storms to the Cape of Good Hope.

Before Jesus, death was the "Cape of Storms" beyond which all was feared lost. No one knew what lay beyond the point of death, except the fear of destruction. But after Jesus was raised from the dead, that changed. The Cape of Storms became the Cape of Good Hope. Jesus went round the horn of death and returned to tell us that on the other side of the storms is God. Now we can see beyond death to the hope that is ours in Jesus Christ. Now, when we round that point into the unknown, we can know that what awaits us is not destruction but eternal life with God. So, the resurrection of Jesus changes the way we look at death.

The resurrection of Jesus also changes the way we look at life. Because Jesus was raised from the dead to new life, we can experience new life too if we place our faith in him. Can you imagine what life would be like without the presence of our risen Savior?

Oh, I suppose some people seem to get along without a vibrant faith in Christ. Some people seem to live decent and happy lives without religious commitments. But those who try to live without God are similar to bushes in the desert. If they have only themselves to rely on, if there is no other source of strength or nourishment, their internal resources will dry up and they will wither away. But those who are connected with God through a living relationship with Jesus Christ are like trees planted by a stream. They know that Jesus is alive. They have a vital relationship with the living Christ who never runs dry, because our resources come from the Living Water that is never exhausted. Because Jesus is alive, we have power for living every day. This does not mean we will be devoid of problems. It does not mean we will never make mistakes. But it does mean that God will give us the resources we need to grow and carry on.

THE REST OF THE STORY, PART 2
(Mark 16:9-20)

Mark 16:9-20 has to be one of the strangest passages in the Bible, even though it begins innocently enough: "Now after he rose early on the first day of the week he appeared to Mary Magdalene" (v. 9). We know the story: it is recorded in John 20.

Mary was at the empty tomb weeping when the risen Jesus appeared to her. She did not recognize him at first. She thought he was the caretaker of the cemetery. But when he called her name, Mary knew it was her Lord. Verses 10-11 tell what happened after that encounter. Mary went and told the disciples (who also were mourning and weeping) that she had seen Jesus alive, but they would not believe her.

"After this he appeared in another form to two of them, as they were walking into the country" (v. 12). We know this story too: it is found in Luke 24. Two disciples were on the road to Emmaus when the risen Jesus appeared to them. They did not recognize him but invited this stranger to have dinner with them. It was only after Jesus took bread and blessed and broke it that they recognized who he was. Verse 13 tells us that these two disciples also went to tell the others what had happened, but the two were met with disbelief.

"Later he appeared to the eleven themselves as they were sitting at the table" (v. 14). This story is also found in Luke 24.

Some of the disciples were still disbelieving, even with the risen Jesus standing there among them. So far, Mark seems to be summarizing some of the Resurrection stories that are recounted in greater detail in Luke and John

"And he said to them, 'Go into all the world and proclaim the good news to the whole creation'" (v. 15). This verse sounds familiar too. It sounds like the Great Commission that Jesus gave his disciples in Matthew 28.

So far, so good. These verses sound like a synopsis of the Resurrection stories in the other three gospels. But then this passage takes a strange turn.

"And these signs will accompany those who believe: by using my name they will cast out demons; they will speak in new tongues; they will pick up snakes in their hands, and if they drink any deadly thing, it will not hurt them; they will lay hands on the sick, and they will recover" (v. 17). Whoa!

Casting out demons, speaking in tongues, handling snakes, drinking poison, laying hands on the sick to heal them—I believe in Jesus, but all those signs are alien to my Christian experience. I have never cast out demons. I don't speak in tongues. I don't handle snakes or drink poison. And, while I regularly pray for the sick and lay hands on them, I don't claim any miraculous healing power. What are we to make of all this?

The last 12 verses in Mark 16 were added to Mark's Gospel sometime after it was written. In all likelihood Mark did not write these verses himself. Most biblical scholars agree that the original text of Mark ends at verse 8. The earliest manuscripts of Mark do not contain verses 9-20. The form, vocabulary, and style of these verses are different from the rest of the book of Mark. Plus, most scholars believe that Mark was the first gospel written, and that Matthew and Luke based their gospels on Mark. Yet verses 9-20 refer to the Resurrection stories in Luke and Matthew and even John. The conclusion of almost every biblical scholar is that these verses were added later to Mark, perhaps during the early second century. Why were they added? There are two reasons.

First, some Christians in the early church were uncomfortable with the gospel of Mark ending with verse 8: "So they went out and fled from the tomb, for terror and amazement had seized them; and they said nothing to anyone, for they were afraid." That was not a good ending to the story of the Resurrection. The women fled in terror and said nothing to anyone: Obviously, there was more to the story than that. The story of the resurrection of Jesus did not end with the women running away from the tomb in terror and saying nothing about it. According to the other gospels, the women went and told the disciples that Jesus was alive. So, verses 9-20 were added to the Gospel of Mark because early Christians did not think the story ended with verse 8. Maybe the last part of Mark's original gospel was lost.

Maybe something happened to Mark, and he was prevented from finishing the story. We don't know. But some Christians in the early second century felt a need to finish the story, so they added these final 12 verses that some Bibles label "The Longer Ending of Mark." There is also a "Shorter Ending of Mark" that was added later.

There is a second reason these verses were added. Whoever wrote them wanted to teach future generations of Christians something about the nature of faith. The author of the longer ending of Mark selected resurrection stories from John, Luke, and Matthew with a common theme: unbelief.

Did you notice that in each case the disciples were unbelieving? Mary told the disciples that she had seen the risen Jesus, but they would not believe it. The two who met the risen Jesus walking on the road told the rest of the disciples what had happened, but they would not believe the two (according to Mark 16:13). The risen Jesus appeared to the 11 disciples as they were sitting at the table, and he upbraided them for their unbelief. That was the typical reaction of Jesus' disciples to his resurrection: unbelief. Those were not the only times the disciples doubted. At the end of Matthew's Gospel, when Jesus appeared to the 11 disciples for the last time and gave them the Great Commission, "they saw him, they worshipped him, but some doubted" (Matt. 28:17). Apparently, some measure of doubt is a part of faith!

I resonate with these stories because I have been something of a religious skeptic my whole life. Even as a child in Sunday School, I can remember questioning some of the stories in the Bible. A talking snake in the Garden of Eden—yeah, right. Two of every kind of animal riding out a great flood on one boat—you've got to be kidding. I used to intimidate my Sunday School teachers because I refused to accept many of the stories in the Bible at face value. I was at once a teacher's dream and a nightmare student: I was a dream student because I really listened and participated; I was a nightmare of a student because I was forever challenging what I was taught. If something did not make sense to me, I said so.

My skepticism might have gotten the better of me and I might have become a total nonbeliever had I not taken an Old Testament survey course in college. During that course I discovered that not everything in the Bible must be interpreted literally. Some of my pious classmates were threatened by that idea, but I found it tremendously liberating.

Not everything in the Bible must be interpreted literally! For example, when Jesus said, "I am the vine and you are the branches," he was not speaking literally. He was using a figure of speech. He was using a metaphor from agriculture to describe his relationship with his disciples. Jesus used parables, analogies, figures of speech, hyperboles, and other literary devices to teach the truth. The truth of the Bible is not confined to a wooden literalism. The nuances of biblical interpretation saved me from rejecting the Bible as nonsense.

I take comfort in the company of fellow skeptics I meet in the Bible. Just about all the disciples were skeptical at first. They were skeptical that Jesus really had come back to life. They doubted the reports of the Resurrection, at first. Some of them still doubted even after seeing the risen Jesus face to face. But instead of arguing with the disciples or trying to convince them that he really was alive, Jesus gave them two things: a purpose to go into all the world and share the good news of salvation and the power to fulfill that purpose.

I think that was what all those signs were about: casting out demons, speaking in tongues, handling snakes, drinking poison without harm, healing the sick. Those were all signs of God's power at work in the lives of Jesus' followers. In the book of Acts, Paul casts out demons and heals the sick and even is bitten by a snake and not harmed, all as evidence of God's power at work in his life. There is nothing in Acts about Paul drinking poison, but there is an early story not in the Bible about a Christian named Justus Barsabbas who drank poison with no ill effect.

Paul also had the gift of speaking in tongues, but he was hesitant to exercise it in deference to those who had not received the gift. As far as we know, many of these signs were not typical of the early church. Nowhere else in the New Testament do we find reference to Christians picking up snakes, although Moses picked up a serpent in the Old Testament. I think the message behind this strange passage is not that every Christian will do these things, but rather that Christians will be filled with the power of the Holy Spirit to fulfill the purpose God has given us.

One of the key principles of biblical interpretation is to never construct an entire theology or system of belief based on one isolated verse in the Bible. And certainly, do not base your beliefs on a verse that was added later to the original text. Not all verses in the Bible are of equal value!

As I said, some measure of doubt is natural and healthy and human. I would have serious doubts about handling snakes or drinking poison or doing other foolish things in the name of faith. When I became a Christian, I did not eviscerate my common sense. But faith also means that there is more to life than rational thinking and common sense. There is a mystery that exceeds our ability to fully understand it. The mystery of faith is what Paul called, "Christ in you, the hope of glory" (Col. 1:27). In a spiritual way, Christ dwells in the heart of every believer. His purpose and his power cause us to live not just for ourselves, but for God.

The longer ending of the Gospel of Mark was one attempt by some Christians in the early second century to finish the story. But maybe Mark did not intend for the story to be finished, even in the second century. Maybe Mark deliberately left his story open-ended. After all, Mark began his gospel with these words: "The beginning of the good news of Jesus Christ, the Son of God" (1:1). Mark was only writing the beginning; the story of the good news of Jesus Christ continues, even today. In your life and in mine, we continue the story of what Jesus has done, and what Jesus continues to do in our world today. God has given each of us a purpose, and the power to fulfill that purpose. God calls us to "go into all the world and proclaim the good news." And God has given us the power to do just that.

The story that Mark began with his gospel is not over. It is up to us to finish it, or at least to write another chapter until Jesus comes again. The last word is not fear and trembling and unbelief. The last word is faith. May God give us the faith to continue with divine purpose and live by God's power until that day when we see our risen Lord face to face and bow down and worship at his throne.

THE UNFINISHED STORY
(Mark 16:9-20)

The fire that destroyed the Village Baptist Church building in January of 2000 also destroyed my pastoral library. Almost immediately after the fire, friends and even people I did not know began to send me books, and eventually the insurance company gave me a check for some of the personal property I lost in the fire. The problem was, I could never completely replace what was lost. Some of the books that burned were out of print, and others were inscribed with a personal message. Most of the books that were destroyed I had read and highlighted and underlined and made notations in, and those could never be replaced. But while I could not replace every volume that was lost, eventually I was able to assemble a collection of roughly equivalent books to rebuild my theological library.

The scripture passage at the end of Mark's Gospel was an attempt to replace what was lost, or at least to replace what appeared to be missing. We do not have the original edition of Mark's Gospel in his own hand, for the best and earliest manuscripts—dating from the fourth century—do not contain verses 9-20 of chapter 16. In fact, the best manuscripts of the Gospel of Mark end with verse 8: "So they went out and fled from the tomb, for terror and amazement had seized them; and they said nothing to anyone, for they were afraid." That was not a good way for the story to end, with the women fleeing from the tomb in terror, and saying nothing to anyone about Jesus rising from the dead. That was a lousy way for the story to end. But in the best manuscripts of Mark, that is the last verse. We don't know why.

We don't know whether Mark intended to end his gospel that way, or whether he was prevented from writing the end to his gospel, or whether he wrote another ending and that part of the gospel was lost. Frankly, it is a mystery why verse 8 is the last verse in the best manuscripts of Mark. It does not seem like that should be the end of the story. We know from the other gospels that the women did go and tell that Jesus had been raised from the dead. Matthew, Luke, and John all contain accounts of the women reporting the Resurrection. So, it does not make sense for Mark not to finish the story that way too.

Apparently, someone in the early church added verses 9-20. From a literary standpoint, it is obvious that these verses were not written by Mark. The style, the grammar, and the vocabulary are all different. Scholars are almost universally agreed that Mark did not write verses 9-20. Not only that, but their content seems to indicate that they were written by someone else. The content seems to be a synthesis, a harmony, a compilation of accounts taken from other parts of the New Testament. It seems obvious that whoever wrote verses 9-20 had access to Matthew and Luke and John, and probably Acts, and perhaps other early Christian writings.

The fact that most of the best manuscripts of Mark do not have verses 9-20 probably means they were not considered scriptural by many ancient authorities. Early Christian scholars such as Eusebius (fourth century) and Jerome (fifth century) rejected this passage as spurious, or nonscriptural. Given the dubious nature of Mark 16:9-20, why is it in the Bible at all? Perhaps it is because it did not seem right for Mark to end with the women running away from the tomb and keeping silent about the Resurrection. Although the longer ending of Mark is not found in the best manuscripts, it is present in the majority of existing

Greek manuscripts. That is why most modern translations have it.

Sadly, some churches even today practice all kinds of bizarre behavior on the basis of verse 17, the one about casting out demons and speaking in tongues and handling snakes and drinking poison. There are still some churches in Appalachia and in other rural areas that practice snake-handling as a part of their worship services, as if it were a test of faith. In my mind, snake-handling and drinking poison are serious misinterpretations of the Bible.

It is dangerous to take one isolated verse out of the Bible and build a whole theology around it. That is a principle to use with regard to any controversial issue. Whether the issue is divorce, or abortion, or capital punishment, or the role of women, or sexual orientation, or war, or money, or countless other issues, it is dangerous to stake out a position on the basis of one verse or a few isolated verses of scripture. We need to understand the entirety of the Bible. We need to study all that the Bible has to say about a particular issue, not just quote one verse or a couple of verses that seem to support a particular point of view. Above all, we need to interpret all the verses of the Bible through the mind and spirit of Christ.

The point of verses 9-20 is that someone has to finish the story. We cannot have Jesus raised from the dead and no one saying anything about it. Someone has to tell the good news. And that is where we fit in. Easter is meaningless if no one says anything about it. If Jesus is raised from the dead and no one says anything about it, does it really matter? Of course, eventually someone did say something about it. Eventually the women did tell others that Jesus had been raised from the dead. Eventually, the word got out, and lives were changed, and the world was changed. But those women are long gone. Who will tell the Easter story today?

Who knows, maybe Mark intended to end with verse 8. Maybe he intended to leave his story unfinished to help us realize that we have a part to play in it. The story is not finished, not by a long shot. Christ is risen! Now, it's up to us to share the good news.

QUESTIONS FOR DISCUSSION/ REFLECTION

1. What do you think about the women who went to Jesus' tomb on Sunday morning?
2. Can you blame the women for being frightened and bewildered?
3. Does verse 8 seem like the end of Mark's Gospel? Why or why not?
4. If you had been at Jesus' tomb that Sunday morning, how would you have reacted?
5. Have there been times when you have been afraid to talk about Jesus?

CHAPTER 4

THE EMPTY TOMB
(Luke 24:1-12)

> *When they returned from the tomb, they reported all these things to the eleven and all the others. Their words struck the apostles as nonsense, and they didn't believe the women. (Luke 24:9, 11 CEB)*

The disciples did not believe the women. Not surprising, since a woman's testimony was not considered reliable. Not surprising, since no one expected Jesus to rise from the dead. What was surprising was that Peter ran to the tomb. Considering that the words of the women struck the apostles as nonsense, why would Peter go to see for himself? Not every ancient manuscript contains the verse about Peter going to the tomb, but some do. The verse may have been added to the original text, based on the account in John 20:3-10. Peter saw that the tomb was empty, but he wondered what had happened. It was hard for all of them to believe that Jesus had been raised.

DEATH WAS ARRESTED
(Luke 24:1-12)

One day when I was serving as pastor at Village Baptist Church in Bowie, Maryland, I received an email from a woman I did not know. She identified herself as Sister Elisabeth. She said she had been trying to reach me, as her earlier emails were returned. Sister Elisabeth identified herself as a Christian, 72 years old, married for 42 years, without a child. She said her doctor told her she had a "cancer problem," and she did not know how long she would be here on this earth. She said that she decided to donate "this little fund" of $3.7 million through me. She wanted me to utilize the money for orphanages, widows, and propagating the word of God. Since she did not have a child to inherit "this little fund," and her husband's relatives were not Christians, she wanted me to take 15 percent of the total for my effort and use 85 percent for the work of God. She said she knew that I would be honest and trustworthy during all my transactions with her. She was expecting to receive my "re-assuring reply." If I calculated correctly, my portion from "this little fund" would have been more than half a million dollars.

Needless to say, I didn't believe a word Sister Elisabeth said. I would have deleted her email, except that I thought it might be a good sermon illustration one day. As all of us know, we cannot trust everything we read on the Internet. A whole new vocabulary of words has been created to describe a variety of Internet scams, for example:

- "catfish"—someone who creates a fake online profile to intentionally deceive
- "phishing"—trying to trick you, often by email, into providing personal data or financial information
- "spear phishing"—phishing with personalized email, often appearing to be from someone you know
- "smishing"—phishing attempts that go to your mobile devices via text message, telling you to call a toll-free number
- "spoofing"—a situation in which a scammer masquerades as a specific person

These words are all part of a "dialect of deception" that is constantly evolving with ever new schemes to take advantage of the unsuspecting.

We cannot believe everything we read on the Internet. We have learned to be skeptical of anything that seems too good to be true, as were the people in Jesus' time. They were especially skeptical of anything said by a woman. Women were not allowed to testify in a court of law, because a woman's word could not be trusted.

It sounds ludicrous, except when you consider how women are treated even today. Let us not forget that for the first 150 years of our nation's history, women were not allowed to vote. Some of us remember when a woman could not apply for a loan or get a credit card in her name. Women continue to be discriminated against around the world. In many countries, women are second-class citizens. In Saudi Arabia, for example, the unofficial ban on women driving automobiles was only recently lifted. According to a reported released in September of 2021 by UN Women, the global wage gap between women and men is 23 percent. In the United States, women earn 79 cents for every dollar a man makes. The U.S. is the only high-income country that does not guarantee paid maternity leave. One in four American mothers must return to work two weeks after giving birth because they are economically unable to stay home and take care of their babies.

Given the status of women today, we should not be surprised that women were considered inferior in Jesus' day. A woman was basically the property of her father or her husband. Yet, Jesus counted many women among his followers. They were among his most loyal disciples. While most of the male disciples were in hiding, some women were present at the foot of the cross when Jesus died. They followed to the tomb and saw where his body was laid. And on Sunday morning, a group of women returned to the tomb with spices they had prepared to give Jesus a proper burial.

At early dawn, they found the stone that had blocked the entrance to the tomb rolled away. The women went into the tomb but did not find his body there. They were trying to figure out what had happened when two figures in dazzling clothes stood beside them. The women were terrified. But the figures said, "Why do you look for the living among the dead? He is not here, but he has risen." They reminded the women how Jesus had told them that on the third day he would rise again.

Returning from the tomb, the women told all this to the 11 disciples and the other followers. This group included Mary Magdalene, Joanna, Mary the mother of James, and other unnamed women who had gone with them. So, there were at least five women, maybe more, who told the apostles that the tomb was empty and Jesus had been raised from the dead. But the apostles did not believe them. The words of the women seemed to them nonsense. To his credit, Peter ran to the tomb to see for himself. But even after stooping and looking in and seeing the grave clothes lying by themselves, he was amazed, yet still not sure what had happened. The words of the women seemed too good to be true.

The apostles doubted the words of the women who came back from the tomb, and people have been doubting their words ever since. We want it to be true, but we have never seen anyone rise from the dead. Was this just an idle tale, or was it something so true that it changes everything?

William E. Hull was the provost and dean of the School of Theology when I entered the Southern Baptist Theological Seminary in Louisville, Kentucky in the fall of 1973. He had a reputation as a brilliant biblical scholar. I came to find out that his commentary on the Gospel of John in the *Broadman Bible Commentary* series remains one of the best. He left the seminary in 1975 to become pastor of the First Baptist Church of Shreveport, Louisiana. In 1987 he returned to the academic world when he became provost and university professor at Samford University in Birmingham, Alabama. The author of some 18 books and a contributor to 24 others, Dr. Hull's reputation only grew after his retirement from Samford in 2000.

Dr. Hull remained active with his writing and speaking, serving as theologian in residence at the Mountain Brook Baptist Church in Birmingham. Then, in 2008, he announced he had been diagnosed with ALS, Lou Gehrig's Disease. ALS is an especially cruel disease, with little treatment and no cure. We all know that we are going to die one day, but most don't know when or how, so we are not confronted with our mortality so immediately. Shortly after he was diagnosed, Dr. Hull preached a sermon at Mountain Brook Church that he titled, "The Darkness That Is Light." In his sermon Dr. Hull said:

> The ultimate issue, therefore, is whether we inhabit one world or two. Is there a realm of both the natural and the supernatural? Of the physical and of the spiritual? Of the temporal and of the eternal? Of the seen and of the unseen? When we pray, are we actually talking to someone other than ourselves?
>
> Which brings us straight to the utterly crucial issue of Jesus. For here was a person who lived simultaneously in two worlds. Because the two domains overlapped, as it were, he lived in earth's present but out of God's future, and called his followers to do the same.
>
> And so the choice is clear. If there are not two worlds, then Jesus was wrong.

After he died on the cross and was buried in the tomb, everyone thought Jesus was wrong. The women went to the tomb to anoint his dead body, but Jesus was not there. When they returned to the disciples with the incredible news that he had risen from the dead, no one believed them. Those who heard the news did not understand that we inhabit not one world, but two.

William Hull died in 2013. At his memorial service at Mountain Brook Church, his family included some quotations from his writings in the printed program. One quotation seemed a fitting summation of his life:

> Easter was not simply the last in an unbroken string of successes, but was rather the astonishing reversal of a series of failures that brought victory only after everything seemed lost. For us, the resurrection of Jesus means that God is willing to work with failure. Our defeats do not daunt or baffle Him.

God is not daunted by failure, or by whatever life may bring. Death does not baffle God. The resurrection of Jesus is promise that nothing can separate us from the love of God.

In the email I received from Sister Elizabeth, she promised me a small fortune. But it was not true. It was nonsense, too good to be true, intended to deceive. But what is true is that God has promised us a gift more valuable than all the fortunes of earth—the gift of eternal life. When Jesus was raised from the dead, God made the down payment on that great gift. This life is not all there is. This world is not all there is. We pray not to an empty sky, but to our loving heavenly Father who raised Jesus from the dead. And through our faith in Jesus, God will raise us up to eternal life.

On her album, *Open Hands*, Laura Story sings: "Our Savior displayed on criminal's cross / Darkness rejoiced as though heaven had lost / But then Jesus arose with our freedom in hand / That's when death was arrested and my life began."

HEAVEN IS FOR REAL
(Luke 24:1-11)

Some years ago, a member of my church loaned me a book. At the time it was #1 on the *New York Times* Best Seller list, with more than 5 million copies in print. She had read it, and she wanted me to read it, so I could let her know what I thought about it. The book was titled, *Heaven Is for Real*, with the intriguing subtitle, *a little boy's astounding story of his trip to heaven and back.*

The book was written by the boy's father, Rev. Todd Burpo, a bivocational pastor of a small evangelical church in Nebraska. The book tells the story of what happened to Todd's son, Colton, when the boy was not yet 4 years old. After recovering from emergency surgery for a burst appendix, young Colton began to describe to his parents what he remembered from the operation. Colton said he remembered sitting in the lap of Jesus, and looking up at the throne of God, and hearing the angels sing "Jesus Loves Me" and "Joshua Fought the Battle of Jericho." Although such stories might be dismissed as nothing more than products of a young boy's vivid imagination, other details that Colton recalled seemed to defy such an easy explanation.

Colton also said he saw his father praying in a small room in another part of the hospital during the operation, a fact his parents had not told him. In addition, Colton said that he met his sister in heaven, which his parents interpreted to mean a miscarriage that his mother had suffered before Colton was born. They had not told him about the miscarriage either. These and other "reminiscences" convinced his parents that Colton had in fact died and gone to heaven during the surgery. Technically, Colton did not die on the operating table, but he may have come close to dying.

What Colton apparently went through is called a "near-death experience." It's not all that uncommon. Many people who have come close to death have survived to tell about what they remember from their experiences. Many of these reports include memories of seeing a bright light, or feeling a sensation of warmth and well-being, or even seeing visions of heavenly beauty.

Another pastor, Don Piper, wrote a book titled *90 Minutes in Heaven*, in which he describes what he remembered after he had been declared dead. What makes the book, *Heaven Is for Real*, so compelling, is that it is told from a child's point of view, and many of the descriptions of heaven reinforce popular images, such as puffy clouds and angels with wings.

I must admit I was skeptical about Colton's story. Even after reading the book, I was not convinced this small boy died and went to heaven and then came back to life. Too many of the details about heaven described in the book sound to me more like the product of the father's imagination than that of his son. I don't think the boy was lying. I think he really believed he saw Jesus and God and the angels, but I also think the father got carried away in trying to interpret what his 4-year-old son was describing. I'm not saying that all near-death experiences are bunk. I'm sure that some people who have come close to death do believe that they saw God or had other spiritual experiences. But my belief in the reality of heaven is not based on the sketchy reminiscences of a 4-year-old boy. My belief in the reality of heaven is based on what happened to Jesus.

We all know the story. Jesus died on the cross on Friday. He was buried in a borrowed tomb before sundown. To prevent anyone from even thinking about stealing his body, a detachment of Roman soldiers was posted as a guard outside the tomb. On Saturday, the Jewish Sabbath, the body of Jesus lay undisturbed in the grave. This was not a near-death experience. Jesus really had died, and no one expected him to come back to life. But early on Sunday morning something miraculous happened.

Matthew's Gospel says there was a great earthquake and an angel descended from heaven and rolled back the stone that had sealed the entrance to the tomb. Matthew also records that the guards fainted at the sight and "became like dead men." The other gospels don't say anything about the guards or the earthquake, but they all agree that when the women arrived at the tomb early that Sunday morning, they found the stone rolled away. Matthew and Mark say there was an angel at the tomb; Luke and John say there were two angels. The four gospels do not agree on every detail of what happened that Sunday morning, but they agree on the basic outline of the story. They all agree that some women came early to the tomb, the stone was rolled away, the body of Jesus was gone, and an angel told them he had been raised from the dead.

Because the four gospels do not agree on every detail, we might wonder if the story is true. Well, like most events, eyewitness accounts can be inconsistent and even contradictory. Who knows exactly what happened in the death of young Trayvon Martin in Florida in 2012? There were no eyewitnesses other than those directly involved. But there was a lot of speculation about what happened. Was it a case of self-defense, as the shooter claimed, or was Trayvon gunned down for no reason other than he was a young black man wearing a hooded sweatshirt? Whatever the circumstances, we should be concerned that Florida's "stand your ground" law encourages anyone to shoot first and ask questions later. Even after the trial, none of us knows for sure what happened. All we know is that Trayvon Martin is dead, and a neighborhood vigilante shot him. And that should make us all weep.

When Jesus died a lot of people wept. But on Sunday morning some women found his grave empty. "Why do you look for the living among the dead?" the angels asked. "He is not here but has risen." Returning from the empty tomb, the women told this to the disciples, but no one believed them. They thought it was nonsense.

There is an interesting theme that runs through the Resurrection stories in all four gospels: hardly anyone believed at first that Jesus really was alive. The disciples didn't believe the women when they said that Jesus had risen from the dead. They thought it was an idle tale. Later that afternoon two disciples were walking on the road to Emmaus, discussing what had happened. The risen Jesus appeared alongside them, but they did not recognize him. With great sadness they talked about the death of Jesus, and how they had hoped in vain that he was the One. They even told about the women going to the tomb and finding it empty. But still they did not believe that Jesus was raised from the dead.

In Mark, the first response of the women is to leave the tomb with great fear and not tell anyone. In John, Mary Magdalene cannot believe that Jesus really is alive. She thinks someone has stolen his body. When the risen Jesus appears to her, she does not recognize him. She assumes he is the caretaker of the garden where the tomb is located. That Sunday night, when the risen Jesus appears to most of the disciples, Thomas isn't there. The others tell him that they have seen the risen Jesus, but Thomas will not believe them. Finally, in Matthew, when the risen Jesus appears to a whole crowd of disciples before he ascends to heaven, even then, some of them doubt. It's a response that runs through each of the four gospels.

The first reaction to the news that Jesus had been raised from the dead was not faith, but doubt. Hardly anyone could believe it at first. Even those who were closest to Jesus had a hard time believing that he really had been raised from the dead.

I take encouragement from the skepticism of these followers of Jesus because his resurrection is hard to believe. It is hard for us to believe that anyone could die and be buried and then on the third day be raised from the dead. In our experience, that just does not happen; death is final. Yes, some people do have near-death experiences, for example, Colton Burpo and Pastor Don Piper and others who were resuscitated after their heart stopped. But for someone to be resurrected from the dead is beyond our experience. It sounds impossible. Yet the New Testament and the Christian faith and our Christian hope are based on the conviction that Jesus really was raised from the dead.

Jesus wasn't just resuscitated after his heart stopped. He didn't come back to life as he was. Yes, his resurrected body was physical, but it was more than physical. His resurrected body could be touched, but it would also appear and disappear and eventually ascend into heaven. Admittedly, this is beyond our experience and our understanding. We've never seen anything like that, and we still find it hard to believe. The first disciples, the ones who knew Jesus personally, found it hard to believe too. Even when they met the risen Jesus face to face some of them doubted. But eventually they became so convinced that Jesus really was alive that they turned the world upside down proclaiming their joyous faith.

The Resurrection means that Jesus was raised from the dead and is still alive, even now! He died on the cross on Friday afternoon and was buried in the tomb before sunset, but on Sunday morning he was raised to life and he lives forevermore. On the night before he died, Jesus told his disciples in the upper room: "Do not let your hearts be troubled. Believe in God, believe also in me. In my Father's house there are many dwelling places…I go to prepare a place for you. And if I go and prepare a place for you, I will come again and will take you to myself, so that where I am, there you may be also" (John 14:1-4). To the penitent thief who was crucified alongside him, Jesus said, "Today, you will be with me in Paradise" (Luke 23:43). Yes, some people have had near-death experiences, and perhaps they even saw a vision of heaven that they remembered enough to tell about. But Jesus really did die, and Jesus really came back, and Jesus has prepared a place in his Father's house for all who place their faith in him.

That's why we know that heaven is for real, not because a little boy had a near-death experience and his father wrote a book about it, but because Jesus was raised from the dead. That's why we feel such joy on Easter Sunday, because the power of God burst the bonds of death and the Resurrection opened the way to live forever in his presence. "For God so loved the world that he gave his only Son so that everyone who believes in him may not perish but may have eternal life" (John 3:16).

I don't suppose anyone on earth knows for sure what heaven is really like. Maybe we will awake to find ourselves sitting in the lap of Jesus and listening to the angels sing. Or maybe we will join in the chorus ourselves, our hearts so filled with joy that we cannot keep from singing. But in the meantime, let us live with joy in our hearts. Let us live today with the assurance that nothing can separate us from the love of God.

This is the message of Easter: Jesus is alive; death is defeated; heaven is for real. We don't have to worry about the past: our sins are forgiven. We don't have to worry about the future: Jesus has gone to prepare a place for us, and he will come again and take us to himself, that where he is, we may be forever. The tomb was empty; the world is full. Our past is forgiven, our future is secure, and today is filled with the presence of our risen Lord. No wonder we sing, "Alleluia!" Doubt your doubts; dare to believe! What if the story is true?

THE THIRD DAY
(Luke 24:1-12)

In his book, *A Doubter's Guide to Heaven*, Terry Giles describes the events that led to his crisis of faith. Devoted Christians, he and his wife Cheryl seemingly were living a charmed life. They had a wonderful marriage and a happy family with three healthy children. Terry had a fulfilling job as a university professor in Erie, Pennsylvania and was the author of several books. Life was good, until that awful day when the doctor came in with the news that Cheryl had cancer. In an instant, their lives were turned upside down. Terry wrote, "The diagnosis of a serious illness can change the way you think. Some things become a whole lot less important, while other issues have an air of immediacy about them." Terry and Cheryl were not prepared for such devastating news. They still had children at home and their whole lives ahead of them. After a few moments of stunned silence, Cheryl simply asked, "Do I have a future?"

Reading their story reminded me of a similar day when my family gathered in a doctor's office in Fort Worth, Texas. My father had not been feeling well for several weeks, and the doctors had run a series of tests that indicated he had cancer. We gathered in the surgeon's office in the hope that an operation would remove the cancer and offer him a chance at healing. After a few anxious moments, the doctor came into the room. The look on his face was not encouraging. He said that the cancer had spread and surgery could not remove it; radiation and chemo were not options either. We were crestfallen. Was there no hope? My father said that he would rather die on the operating table than do nothing. But the doctor replied that surgery would only make it worse. We drove back to my parents' home that afternoon in stunned silence. It is almost unbearable to live without hope.

The disciples felt that way after Jesus died on the cross. They were crestfallen and brokenhearted. They gathered in stunned silence. Their dreams were shattered, and their hope was gone. Then the women came back from the tomb on Sunday morning with unbelievable news: Jesus had been raised from the dead. The disciples did not believe them. The words of the women seemed like an idle tale. Yet, Peter set aside his disbelief. He ran to the tomb, with doubt in his mind, but hope in his heart.

In the movie, *The Shawshank Redemption*, the two central characters have a continuing disagreement about hope. Tim Robbins and Morgan Freeman play two prisoners in a state penitentiary. The character played by Morgan Freeman has been in prison a long time, and he has learned to manage the daily disappointments of life by giving up hope. The character played by Tim Robbins has been more recently incarcerated, convicted of a crime he did not commit. At one point, Freeman says to Robbins, "Hope is a dangerous thing. Hope can break your heart." But for Robbins, to give up hope is to give in to despair. For Robbins, hope is the only thing that gives him a reason to live.

As Peter ran to the tomb that Sunday morning, he must have wondered if he was only setting himself up for more disappointment and devastation. Doubt can crush your spirit, but unfulfilled hope can break your heart. What the women had told the disciples sounded impossible, but after having lost Jesus, what more did Peter have to lose? So, Peter kept running, until he reached the tomb. Then stooping and looking inside, he saw the burial cloths lying by themselves. The body of Jesus was not there. Perplexed and amazed, Peter returned home. He was not a believer, yet, but his doubts were giving way to hope. Maybe, just maybe, it was true.

On the day that Jesus died, all hope seemed lost. Just as he had prayed from the cross, Jesus did seem to be forsaken by God. An innocent man died a horrible death. And when they laid his body in the tomb, it seemed it was all over. It seemed his life did not mean a thing, that all he had said and done had been for naught. That was day number one: a dark day that faded into a darker night.

Day number two was no better. Day two was Saturday, the Jewish Sabbath. No work could be done on that day. The women could not even go to the tomb to mourn. They would have to be still and silent and wait. They were grieving, but they could not do anything to express their sorrow or to assuage their grief. Sometimes the hardest thing to do is to do nothing. That was Saturday, day number two.

But a third day was coming, and on the third day everything changed. The women approached Jesus' tomb just before dawn on Sunday morning, bringing the spices they had prepared to anoint the body. Jesus had been buried with such haste that he had not been given a proper burial. So, the women came to the tomb before daybreak fully expecting to find his lifeless body there. But when they arrived, they found that the stone blocking the entrance to the tomb had been rolled away. And when they went into the tomb, they did not find his body. As they stood there perplexed, wondering what this could mean, suddenly two figures in dazzling clothes stood beside them. "Why do you look for the living among the dead?" they asked the women. "He is not here but has risen. Remember how he told you that the Son of man must be handed over to sinners, and be crucified, and on the third day rise again." The third day—yes, the third day changes everything!

You and I live in a "first day" world, or at best a "second day" world. Things get messed up. Bad things happen. People get cancer. Workers lose their jobs. Families lose their homes. Marriages come to an end. Sooner or later death comes knocking at the door. We live in a first-day world where terrible things happen, or at best a second-day world, where we feel powerless to do anything about them. But the third day is coming.

The third day is one of hope. The third day is when the stone gets rolled away and when the tomb gets opened. The third day is when God raised Jesus from the dead; it is God's day, the Lord's Day. That was why the early Christians began to worship on Sunday instead of on the Jewish Sabbath. The Sabbath began on Friday night and lasted until sundown on Saturday. Those were days one and two—the day that Jesus died, and the day that Jesus lay in the tomb. Day one and day two are dark days. But there is a third day, and Christians are a third-day people. We worship a third-day God. Jesus is our third-day Lord.

John Ortberg, in his book *Faith & Doubt*, writes, "Just as bats have radar and dogs hear whistles, we have moments when it is clear to us that 'things are not what they seem.'" What if it really is true? What if the tomb really was empty? What if Jesus really was raised from the dead? Well, that changes everything.

This world is not all there is. This life is not all there is. There is more than meets the eye, more than we can understand. Jesus was right all along: The kingdom of heaven is at hand. The joy of our salvation is near. The deepest longing of our hearts is not wishful thinking but echoes of immortality. The grave is not our final destination. Death is not the end of life. We were created for a destiny beyond the bounds of earth and time. This world is not our home.

Now, the third day does not eliminate days one and two. Bad things still happen in a first-day world. Innocent people still suffer. Sometimes cancer comes. Sometimes the job is terminated. Sometimes the marriage ends. Sometimes death knocks far too soon. But heartache, sorrow, and loss are not the final words. Death is not the final word.

When Cheryl Giles was told that she had cancer, she had only one question: "Do I have a future?" That is the eternal question of the human heart, for all of us have been given a death sentence. If not cancer, then something else—all of us sooner or later will die. But do we have a future?

On the third day God answered that eternal question of the human heart with a resounding, "YES!" When God raised Jesus from the dead, he offered hope to every human heart. Of course, we all will die, some sooner, some later. But we have a future. God raised Jesus from death, and God will give new life to every person who believes in him. We have a future because this life is not all there is, and a third day is coming.

Martin Heidegger, the 20th-century philosopher, said that what we believe about the future is important because it affects how we live in the present. If we don't believe we have a future, then it really does not matter what we do in the present. But if we do believe we have a future, then that affects the way we choose to live right now. Young people go to school because they believe education will help them prepare for a job. Workers invest in an IRA or 401(k) account because they believe that one day they can use that money in retirement. Christians lay up for ourselves not just treasures on earth, but treasures in heaven, because we believe that we have a future beyond this earth with God. What we believe about the future helps determine the way we live today.

Jesus was raised on the third day, and that is our hope, that a third day is coming for us too. No one knows what the future holds, but we know who holds the future. No one knows what tomorrow may bring, but we have hope because every tomorrow belongs to God. Do we have a future? Yes, and our future is in God's hands.

When my father was given a death sentence it was almost more than we could bear. To watch a loved one die, and to be able to do absolutely nothing about it, is a helpless feeling. But even then, we were not without hope. Jesus was raised from the dead by the power of God. Because of Jesus, death is not the end of life, but the beginning of a new and greater and eternal life with God. The third day changes everything.

QUESTIONS FOR DISCUSSION REFLECTION

1. Reflect upon the role of women in the Easter story. What does it say about the role of women in the church today?
2. Why was no one expecting Jesus' resurrection?
3. Why did the disciples not believe the women's report?
4. What is the role of Peter in the Easter story?
5. What hope does the Resurrection story give us?

CHAPTER 5

THE ROAD TO EMMAUS
(Luke 24:13-35)

On that same day, two disciples were traveling to a village called Emmaus. Jesus himself arrived and joined them on their journey. They were prevented from recognizing him.
(Luke 24:13a, 15b, 16 CEB)

The risen Jesus appeared to two disciples on the road to Emmaus. It was same day that Jesus had been resurrected from the dead, but Cleopas and the other disciple did not recognize him. They thought he was just another visitor to Jerusalem who was heading back home. The two disciples knew that something had happened. They were stunned by the reports of the women who had gone to the tomb early that morning. They knew that others from their group had gone to the tomb to check out the women's story, and found that Jesus wasn't there. Still, when Jesus appeared alongside them, they did not know who he was.

As they walked along together, Jesus explained to the two disciples that what had happened was the fulfillment of prophecy. When they came to Emmaus it appeared as if Jesus were going on. The two disciples invited him to stay with them. As they sat together at the table, Jesus assumed the role of the host, taking the bread, blessing and breaking it, and giving it to them. At that moment, their eyes were opened, and they recognized who he was. Then he disappeared from their sight. They remarked to each other, "Weren't our hearts on fire when he spoke to us along the road and when he explained the scriptures for us?" Returning to Jerusalem, the two found the other followers of Jesus who had gathered. The others were saying, "The Lord really has risen! He appeared to Simon!" Then the two told what had happened to them and how Jesus had been made known to them in the breaking of the bread.

THE WALK TO EMMAUS
(Luke 24:13-35)

The story of the walk to Emmaus is one of my favorites in the Bible. I've preached on it at least half a dozen times, and every time I come back to it, there is still more to learn, and more to think about, and more to say. There is a lot about this story we don't know. First, we don't know who these people were. Who was Cleopas? Who was his unnamed companion? All we know is that they were followers of Jesus.

Second, we don't know exactly where they were going, because we don't know exactly where Emmaus was, only that it was located about seven miles outside of Jerusalem. Apparently, Emmaus was such an obscure place, so small and insignificant, that no one bothered to record its precise location.

Third, we don't know why the risen Jesus appeared to these two travelers that Sunday afternoon after the Resurrection. We know from John's Gospel that Jesus already had appeared to Mary Magdalene in the garden beside the tomb. We know from Matthew's Gospel that the risen Jesus appeared to the women as they left the tomb. We know from Luke's Gospel that Jesus appeared to Peter sometime that day, and that he would appear to most of the 11 remaining disciples later that night. But why Jesus appeared to these two on the road to Emmaus we cannot say. These two were not members of his inner circle of disciples. Some scholars speculate that it might have been the wife of Cleopas since they invited Jesus to stay with them once they reached their home in Emmaus.

The fact that we know so little about the details of this story makes it all the more intriguing. It was Sunday afternoon, and the two travelers were on their way home. They were talking about what had happened the past few days, how Jesus had been handed over by the chief priests to be condemned to death. They had hoped he was the one who would redeem Israel, but now they weren't so sure.

Yes, there was the report of the women that had astounded them. The women had said that when they went to the tomb early in the morning, they found it empty. The women returned to the disciples and told them about seeing a vision of angels. Some of the other disciples ran to the tomb to see for themselves. But these two had pretty much given up hope and were on their way home. The risen Jesus came alongside them on the road, but they did not recognize who he was. As they walked and talked, Jesus asked them why they were so sad. "Are you the only stranger in Jerusalem who doesn't know what happened?" they asked. As they continued along, Jesus used the scriptures to interpret to them what they did not yet understand.

As they neared the village of Emmaus, Jesus walked ahead of the two travelers—as if he were going on—but they urged him to come in and stay with them. Jesus accepted their hospitality. As they sat down at the table, Jesus took bread and blessed and broke it and gave it to them. That's when their eyes were opened; that's when they recognized who he was. Just at that moment, he vanished from their sight. The astonished disciples said to each other, "We should have known it. Were not our hearts burning within us while he was talking to us on the road, while he was explaining the scriptures to us?" They got up and rushed back to Jerusalem to tell the others what had happened on the road, and how Jesus was made known to them in the breaking of the bread.

I suppose there are many points to this story, but the one that impresses me is that the risen Jesus made himself known only to those who loved him and were grieving his death. As far as we know, Jesus did not appear to his enemies after the Resurrection, but he did appear to his friends. He did not remain with them for long in visible form, but he was with them long enough to let them know that he was alive. And that is the promise of Easter down to this day: Jesus is alive, and he is with us even now. Of course, Jesus does not appear to us in visible form. Even if he did, how could we recognize him? We don't know what he looked like. All we have are imaginary pictures in our minds of what he might have looked like. Unlike those to whom he did appear, we would not be able to identify him because we never saw him. So, in this sense the Resurrection appearances recorded in the Bible were unique.

But this we do share with those who saw Jesus face to face. We share the belief that Jesus is still with us, in a spiritual way. And we can experience his spiritual presence even today. It's not a question of doing something to summon him. The risen Christ is with us all the time. But we are not aware of his presence all the time. Most of the time, our minds are set on other things. Most of the time, our awareness is focused on more mundane preoccupations. But how much richer and powerful and peaceful would our lives be if we were more aware of the presence of our risen Lord in every moment?

The walk to Emmaus is a paradigm for how we can become more aware of the presence of the risen Christ in our lives. First, notice that their hearts burned within them as Jesus opened to them the scriptures. We can become more aware of Christ's presence in our lives as we read and study the Bible. In many and various ways, the scriptures point us to Jesus.

One of the blessings of being a pastor (and even a retired pastor now) is that I read the Bible every day. Much of that reading was related to my profession. As I would often say, Sunday's coming and people expect me to have some word from the Lord. So, reading and studying the Bible was a part of my ministry and my identity. But one of the reasons I felt called into the ministry in the first place was my love of the scriptures. Reading the Bible has not been a chore or an obligation for me; it's an adventure and a joy. It's an adventure to learn more about God, and it's a joy to encounter the risen Jesus time and again through God's holy word.

Village Baptist Church supports several missionaries involved in translating the Bible into other languages. Katherine Cooper and her husband Rolf Buehler are Wycliffe Bible translators, and much of their work involves scripture translation in Africa. Cooperative Baptist Fellowship missionaries Keith Holmes and Mary van Rheenen serve in Eastern Europe, where Keith is involved with making audio scripture recordings in various dialects of the Roma languages. Another CBF missionary couple, Shane and Dianne McNary, work with a scripture translation nonprofit in Slovakia called Word for the World. Shane has served on the board of directors of the organization, which translates the Bible into a local dialect of the Roma language. The New Testament is complete, and they are making audio recordings of the Old Testament. Why would these missionaries devote so much of their efforts into translating the Bible into other languages? Why? Because people encounter the risen Christ through the scriptures.

A second way that we can encounter the risen Christ is through our fellowship with other believers. It was only when they sat down together to share a meal that the two believers in Emmaus recognized the risen Jesus in their midst. The scene almost has communion overtones. It was when Jesus took bread and blessed and broke it and gave it to the two travelers that they recognized who he was. Surely, every time we share the Lord's Supper we are reminded that the risen Christ is with us. But it's not just during communion that we become aware of his presence. Any meal among fellow believers can make us aware of Christ's presence. That's why we gather from time to time in church to share a meal. We encounter the risen Christ when we eat together, whether it be a church dinner or the Lord's Supper.

A third way that we can encounter the risen Christ is through Christian hospitality. Notice that the two on the road to Emmaus invited the stranger to stay with them even before they knew who he was. Jesus said that whenever we extend hospitality to the "least of these," we do it to him.

When I was pastor of Village Baptist Church, every year our church extended hospitality to some homeless guests through our Warm Nights ministry. About 30 homeless guests stayed in our church building every night for a week, beginning on Sunday night. I recall one year when there was a family with three young children. On Monday, the church secretary, Bev, and I were working in our offices when a school bus pulled up in front of the church. I watched as the bus monitor escorted a little boy to the front door of our building. I didn't know who the boy was, but I guessed that he was one of our homeless guests. I asked him, "Did you stay here last night?" He nodded his head and said yes. For a moment, I wasn't sure what to do. Unattended children were not supposed to be dropped off at the church. Either his parents should have been there to meet him, or the bus should have taken him where his parents were.

While the bus monitor and the little boy waited in the foyer, I called Donny at Community Crisis Services, the organization that managed the Warm Nights program. Donny said there was no protocol for children dropped off at the church by a school bus. While I was talking with Donny, Bev was talking with the bus driver. He had a phone number for the little boy's parents, and Bev was able to contact them. She and I agreed that the boy could stay with us until his parents could come to pick him up. So, the bus driver and the bus monitor left him in our care while they continued on their bus route delivering other children to their homes.

Bev rounded up some paper and markers so the little boy could draw pictures while he waited for someone to come get him. About half an hour later, his father arrived in a taxi. It would be hard to overstate how glad the little guy was to see his father coming up the front steps. The family stayed with us several more nights during the week until CCSI (Coordinated Care Services Inc.) was able to arrange for transitional housing for them. But the face of that little boy became for me the face of homelessness, and in a way, the face of Jesus too. Yes, the risen Jesus was surely among us that week of Warm Nights. Whatever we did for the least of these, we did for him.

So, you see, Jesus really is among us. We don't see him in a physical way, but we encounter his spiritual presence as we read the scriptures and share fellowship with one another and serve others in his name. The risen Jesus came alongside the disciples as they walked the road to Emmaus. The risen Jesus comes alongside us on the roads we travel, and he will journey with us all the way home.

BREAKING OF THE BREAD
(Luke 24:13-35)

"He was made known to them in the breaking of the bread." That's how the two disciples going to Emmaus recognized the risen Jesus. When Jesus took bread and blessed and broke it, they knew who he was. It sounds like communion. "He was made known in the breaking of the bread."

One Good Friday I was moving a large wooden cross from my church's sanctuary into the narthex. The cross had been in the shadows behind the baptistery for our Maundy Thursday service. But on Good Friday I carried the cross on my back from behind the baptistery down the center aisle of the sanctuary and out into the foyer. Carrying the cross was my own way of remembering the Way of Sorrows that Jesus walked on Good Friday as he carried his cross. But beyond the devotional aspect of it, there was a practical purpose. Members of the Flower Committee were coming in on Saturday morning to decorate for Easter, and they needed the cross in the foyer as the focal point for their placement of flowers there.

The wooden cross was about eight feet tall and fit into a base so that it could stand upright. After I had carried the cross into the foyer and laid it down, I went back behind the baptistery to retrieve the base. As I was stationing the base in the middle of the window in the foyer, I backed up to make sure it was centered. I was so focused on getting the stand situated that I forgot I had laid the cross down on the floor. As I was backing up, I tripped over the cross and lost my balance. I was carrying a couple of small planks of wood that were used to stabilize the cross in the base. Fortunately, I had enough sense to fling those planks of wood out of my hands as I was falling, so I could brace myself when I hit the floor. It happened in a split second, but it felt like I was falling in slow motion; I could do nothing about it other than prepare myself to crash.

As I lay on the floor, my first instinct was to look around and make sure no one had seen me fall. It was embarrassing enough to take a tumble by myself. It would have been even more humiliating had someone seen me go down and lie sprawled out like that. Fortunately, no one was around. Even more fortunately, I was not seriously hurt. I did twist my knee as I tried to keep myself from falling, but other than hobbling around for a week, I suffered no major injury—except to my pride. The only consolation is that I'm not the first person to get tripped up by the cross. In 1 Corinthians 1:23 Paul wrote, "but we proclaim Christ crucified, a stumbling block to Jews and foolishness to Gentiles, but to those who are called, both Jews and Greeks, Christ the power of God and the wisdom of God."

The Cross has always been a stumbling block to faith. To both Jews and Greeks, the death of Jesus seemed to be the end not only of Jesus, but also of his movement. The Cross seemed to be a sign of failure and defeat. Who in his right mind would have faith in a teacher who had been crucified?

My wife Linda and I watched *The Bible* mini-series on the History Channel. The final episode depicted the Crucifixion of Jesus. It was almost too graphic to watch. Mel Gibson's movie, *The Passion of the Christ*, was even more graphic. Both of these films portray the Crucifixion as deliberately horrible. It was designed to be as humiliating and painful as possible. No wonder the Cross was a stumbling block to Jews and Greeks alike. For Jesus to die in such humiliation and agony was the essence of defeat. That's why the two disciples on the road to Emmaus that Sunday afternoon were so dejected. They had hoped Jesus was the one to redeem Israel. Instead, he had suffered a degrading and despicable death.

The death of Jesus on the cross made no sense at the time. But then came Sunday morning. After Jesus was raised from the dead, his followers came to recognize the cross not as a sign of defeat but as a sign of victory. Through his death on the cross, Jesus forgave all our sins. Yet, without the Resurrection, his death would mean nothing other than a miscarriage of justice and another example of the triumph of sin in our world.

On Monday of that same Holy Week when I stumbled over the cross, I was summoned to the courthouse in Upper Marlboro, Maryland for jury duty. My summons was for one day or one trial. After orientation I was appointed to a panel of 65 potential jurors. We were escorted into a courtroom for the trial of a young man accused of armed robbery at a Metro station. There were so many potential jurors in the courtroom that we filled up every available seat and the bailiff had to bring in additional chairs. I wondered why it was necessary to have a pool of 65 potential jurors, since only 12 jurors and two alternates were required. It took a while, but eventually I understood.

After many preliminary instructions, the judge asked if any of the potential jurors had ever been arrested, convicted of a crime, or were the victim of a crime. All those who could answer yes to the question were asked to stand. I was astonished that most of the potential jurors in the courtroom stood. Each of those who stood was asked to approach the bench individually and tell the judge, the attorneys, and the defendant why he or she had stood. Either they had been arrested for a crime, convicted of a crime, or were the victim of a crime.

Out of 65 potential jurors, 46 approached the bench. I was seated on the back row of the jury box. Out of the eight people seated on my row, I was the only one who did not stand and the only one who did not approach the bench and explain my circumstances to the judge. Of those 46 who were accused of crimes or were victims of crimes, many of them were dismissed from serving on that jury, either by the defense attorney or the prosecuting attorney or the judge. Now I understood why they needed 65 potential jurors for that trial. Apparently so many people in Prince George's County have had a brush with the law or have been crime victims that choosing impartial jurors is a lot more complicated than it might seem.

My experience at the courthouse reminded me of the reality of sin in our world. More than two-thirds of the jurors had a history of some type of criminal activity, either as perpetrators or victims. It also reminded me that I lead a rather sheltered life. I have never been arrested for a crime, and I have never been the victim of a serious crime. I've had people steal from me, but no one was arrested. Most of the folks I deal with are "good Christian people." Most of my friends go to church. Most of my business dealings are with reputable, upstanding citizens. My life is insulated from criminal activity. That was one of the blessings of being a pastor. My faith and my vocation were intertwined. About the only day I was not immersed in spiritual matters was Thursday when I played golf. But most of the fellows I played golf with were Baptist ministers, so even then, I was sheltered from the "real world."

Most people are not like me. Most people live in the real world. They don't spend every day in church. They may go to church on Sundays, but most of their time is spent in nonreligious settings. This story about the disciples on the road to Emmaus is especially for them. Those two disciples experienced the presence of the risen Christ not in the temple, not in the synagogue, not in church, but in their everyday life. They were on their way back home when a stranger appeared alongside them on the road. They didn't recognize him until they invited him in for dinner. Then, in the breaking of the bread, they knew who he was.

This is the message: The spirit of the risen Jesus is present not only in church, but also in the everyday circumstances of our lives. Every time we break bread, Christ is with us. Whether it's communion at church or an ordinary meal someplace else, the spirit of the risen Christ is with us. This spirit is present in church, yes, but it is also present in the real world where we do most of our living. Why then do we need to go to church? Well, we go to church to be reminded that Jesus Christ is with us in spirit. Gathering with other believers, praying and reading scripture together, and sharing the Lord's Supper—all remind us that Jesus is with us in spirit. It's easy to forget about that in the real world.

Even though I spent a long time in the courtroom when I was called for jury duty, I did not serve on a jury the day of my summons. Enough other potential jurors were deemed qualified that my number was not called, and I got to go home after only five hours in the courthouse. I don't know what happened to that defendant accused of armed robbery at a Metro station. Maybe he was guilty, but maybe not. But I know that all of us are guilty before God, yet Jesus paid our debt and set us free. And I do know that the spirit of the risen Jesus is with us, whether as a stranger on the road or in the breaking of the bread.

THE BACK ROADS OF LIFE
(Luke 24:13-35)

Linda and I have been blessed to take some special vacation trips. We went to Ireland to celebrate our 20th wedding anniversary. We went to British Columbia in Canada with my parents to see where my father was born. We went to northern California after visiting our daughter Amy when she was living in Los Angeles. We went to Wisconsin, again with my parents, to the Green Lake Conference Center. For our 25th wedding anniversary we used our credit card frequent flyer miles to go to Hawaii. Just about everywhere we have gone, we have found that some of our most memorable experiences came when we got off the main highway and traveled the back roads.

In Ireland, there aren't that many main highways to begin with, but while traveling the back roads we happened upon some ancient ruins that left indelible impressions on our minds. In one instance we came to the site of an abandoned monastery, well over a thousand years old. At first, we were disappointed because the gate in the stone wall surrounding the monastery was locked. But then we noticed a hole in the wall big enough to step through. We stepped through the hole and followed a worn path to the ruins of an ancient church. In the center of the church was a stone cross, maybe 15 feet tall, with biblical scenes carved into all four sides, from top to bottom. For a time, we were the only people there, until other tourists discovered the hole in the wall and followed the worn path to see for themselves.

When we were traveling through British Columbia, we deliberately got off the main highway to take back roads through the rugged mountains and pristine forests. Along many miles there were no signs of civilization except for the paved road itself—no telephone poles, no electric wires, no advertising signs, just thousands and thousands of trees growing so close together it was like a wall of pines on either side. For a stretch of our journey, we drove over a gravel road. We came to a little town named Lytton. Seeing on the map that it would be our last chance to get something to eat for a while, we stopped at the only restaurant in town, which was located in the only hotel in town. To call it a "dining room" is a bit generous. The carpeting on the floor looked like it had been there half a century. After we had placed our order, we noticed that we were the only Caucasians there. Everyone else, both patrons and staff, were Native Americans, or perhaps I should say Native Canadians. We felt a little conspicuous being the only "white people" in the entire place. But once again, it was an experience we will never forget.

The common thread of our travels has been that some of our most memorable experiences have come as we have gotten off the main highways and traveled the back roads. When we were in Wisconsin, staying at the American Baptist Assembly grounds, I picked up a book of poetry written by Lawrence Janssen, an American Baptist minister. Janssen served as a staff member of the American Baptist Home Mission Society, and in that role he had the opportunity to travel extensively throughout North and Central America, from Alaska to Puerto Rico, from Maine to Nicaragua, and in Canada from Vancouver Island to Nova Scotia. Later Janssen served as program director of the American Baptist Assembly at Green Lake. One of his poems provided inspiration for this message. I even borrowed the title, "The Back Roads of Life."

Janssen loved the beauties of nature, and he sponsored many seminars and workshops on what it means to be good stewards of the earth. But he also had an appreciation for the people he met on the back roads of life. In his poem he wrote,

> I've hurried here, I've hurried there,
> pushed and pulled by need and care.
> But the best of what I cherish now
> I've learned as I traveled the back roads of life.

In Luke 24 we read about one of those back roads of life. It was Sunday, and two disciples were on their way back home to a little village called Emmaus. They were walking along a back road, both literally and figuratively. The road to Emmaus was a literal back road because we don't know where Emmaus was. It was such an obscure place that its precise location is unknown today. All we know is that Emmaus was about seven miles from Jerusalem—which direction from Jerusalem we do not know. Scholars have suggested at least four modern-day sites that may have been the location of the ancient village of Emmaus. Apparently, it was such an unimportant town that no one remembers where it was located. In that respect, the road to Emmaus was a literal back road.

The road to Emmaus also was a figurative back road for the two disciples. It was an emotional and spiritual low point in their lives. They were returning home from Jerusalem with heavy hearts. They were talking with one another about what had happened just days before, how Jesus, a prophet mighty in word and deed, had been handed over to the chief priests and then had been condemned to death and crucified. To compound their grief and confusion, some of the women in the group of disciples had gone to the tomb early on Sunday morning and found it empty. They had seen a vision of angels who told them that Jesus was alive. Some of the incredulous disciples had gone to the tomb themselves and found it just as the women said, but they did not see Jesus. So, these two disciples apparently assumed it was all just some kind of cruel hoax, and they were on their way back home, back to Emmaus, back to the obscure little village so they could get on with their mundane lives.

Suddenly, as the two disciples were talking and walking along that back road, Jesus came alongside them, but they did not recognize him. Perhaps they had dismissed the possibility that Jesus could be alive. Sometimes when I run into someone in another context, someone I am not expecting to see, I will not recognize that person at first. But this was a common theme in many of the Resurrection stories: the disciples of Jesus did not recognize him at first. Perhaps his appearance was somehow changed by the Resurrection, or perhaps the disciples were so blinded by their own grief or disappointment that they were not expecting to see him. In any case, Jesus appeared and walked with the two disciples along that back road to Emmaus, but they did not know who he was. As they walked along, they shared with Jesus all that had happened, and Jesus shared with them what all those things meant as he interpreted the scriptures for them.

When the two disciples came to the village of Emmaus, Jesus appeared to be traveling on but they urged him to come in and stay the evening with them. It was dangerous to travel at night, especially alone on a back road. Jesus accepted their invitation. As they were seated at the table for the evening meal, Jesus the guest assumed the role of the host. He took bread and blessed and broke it and gave it to them. At once their eyes were opened and they recognized him, but then he vanished out of their sight. They said to one another, "Were not our hearts burning within us while he was talking to us on the road, while he was opening the scriptures to us?" Then they rushed back to Jerusalem, walking the seven miles on that back road in the dark of the night, to tell the other disciples how Jesus had been made known to them on the road, through the scriptures, and in the breaking of bread.

You and I did not have the privilege and the blessing of knowing Jesus in the flesh as did those first disciples, but Jesus still makes himself known on the back roads of life. Jesus still makes himself known through the scriptures and the breaking of bread. If we are sensitive to his presence, we will recognize that our risen Lord still comes to us in the everyday events and ordinary experiences of our lives. The truth is that most of our lives are traveled on the back roads rather than on the major highways. Going to work or school or the store, running errands, even attending church: these are mundane, back-road experiences that fill most of our days.

Most of life is lived on the back roads. And the good news is that Jesus comes to us on the back roads of life to walk with us on our journey. Jesus may come when we least expect him, but the risen Christ appears, if we have eyes and hearts to see him, on the back roads of life. "I will never leave you or forsake you," Jesus said. He hasn't, and he won't, no matter where the back roads may take us. In fact, it is on the back roads of life that he comes most near.

QUESTIONS FOR DISCUSSION/REFLECTION

1. Where is the "road to Emmaus" in your life?
2. Has Jesus ever joined you on your journey when you were not expecting it?
3. In what ways is Jesus present in "the breaking of bread"?
4. In what other ways is Jesus present to us?
5. When has Jesus changed your mourning to joy?

CHAPTER 6

JESUS APPEARS TO HIS DISCIPLES
(Luke 24:36-49)

> *Jesus himself stood among them and said to them, "Peace be with you." They were startled and frightened, thinking they saw a ghost. He showed them his hands and his feet. And while they still did not believe it because of joy and amazement, he asked them, "Do you have anything here to eat?" (Luke 24:36b-37, 40b-41 NIV)*

They thought he was a ghost. The disciples who had gathered in Jerusalem had just heard the report from Cleopas and his companion about their encounter with the risen Jesus on the road to Emmaus. After recognizing Jesus in the breaking of bread, and having Jesus vanish from their sight, the two had rushed back to Jerusalem to tell the other disciples about it. By now the others knew that Jesus had risen, for he had appeared to Simon. Still, they did not understand the corporal nature of Jesus' resurrection. They thought he was a ghost.

So, when Jesus appeared to all of them, he invited the disciples to look at his hands and his feet and to touch him. There was joy, yet still disbelief. So, Jesus demonstrated that he was not a ghost by eating a piece of fish in their presence. Then Jesus explained how his suffering and resurrection were the fulfillment of scripture. His commissioning of them to proclaim repentance and the forgiveness of sins in his name to all the nations anticipates Luke's second volume, the Acts of the Apostles. Likewise, Jesus' instruction to remain in the city until they had been clothed with power from on high anticipates what would happen on the day of Pentecostas as recorded in Acts. Jesus was not a ghost! He was, and is, alive!

WHAT'S THE LEAST I CAN BELIEVE?
(Luke 24:36-49)

Martin Thielen, a retired minister in the Methodist Church, once met a man who identified himself as an unbeliever. Upon their first meeting the man said quite bluntly: "Preacher, you need to know that I'm an atheist. I don't believe the Bible. I don't like organized religion. And I can't stand self-righteous, judgmental Christians." Despite their considerable differences, the man's avowed atheism and Martin's devout Christian faith, they became friends.

Over the next year or so Martin and his friend had many spirited conversations about what they did and did not believe. Gradually, Martin's friend began to rethink his belief system and to soften his rhetoric. One day he announced with a chuckle, "I've decided to upgrade from atheist to agnostic." Several months later his friend said, "I've had an epiphany. I realize that I don't reject Christianity. Instead, I reject the way intolerant Christians package Christianity." A few weeks later his friend said, "Martin, you've just about convinced me on this religion stuff. So I want to know: What's the least I can believe and still be a Christian?"

Martin Thielen wrote a book with that intriguing title, *What's the Least I Can Believe and Still Be a Christian?* Over the years as a pastor, he had encountered many false ideas that misrepresent what the Christian faith is all about. He calls these false ideas "close-minded faith." So, in the first part of his book he gives specific examples of some false ideas that Christians don't need to believe.

For instance, we don't need to believe that God causes cancer, or car wrecks, or catastrophes. We don't need to believe that women can't be preachers and must submit to the authority of men. We don't need to believe that everything in the Bible should be taken literally. We don't need to believe that God loves straight people but hates gay people. These and many other false and "close-minded" ideas have given Christianity a bad name. As a result, many people have given up on organized religion or written off the church altogether.

A few years ago, *Time* magazine reported that "the fastest growing religious group in the U.S. is the category of people who say they have no religious affiliation" at all. *Time* referred to these people as "the Nones."[1] The number of people who say they have no religious affiliation has greatly increased, to more than a quarter of the U.S. population.[2] It's not that all these people have given up on God. Only 4 percent of Americans describe themselves as atheist or even agnostic. But they have given up on organized religion, which they perceive to be self-righteous, hypocritical, intolerant, and judgmental. These "nones" sometimes describe themselves as spiritual, but not religious.

A *Newsweek* cover story a few years ago had an image of a modern-day Christ, with the caption, "Forget the Church: Follow Jesus." The author of the story, Andrew Sullivan, wrote that "Christianity has been destroyed by politics, priests, and get-rich evangelists." Sullivan advised, "Ignore them, and embrace Him" (Jesus).[3] According to both the *Time* and *Newsweek* articles, people are increasingly giving up on the institutional church and doing their own thing when it comes to spirituality. I can understand the disillusionment. There are a lot of churches I would stay away from. Any time someone tries to tell me what I must believe, I tend to go the other way.

Martin Thielen, the Methodist minister who wrote the book *What's the Least I Can Believe and Still Be a Christian?* grew up as a Southern Baptist. He made his profession of faith in a Southern Baptist church, graduated from a Southern Baptist college, and received theological degrees from two Southern Baptist seminaries. He served as pastor of several Southern Baptist churches and as an editor for the Southern Baptist Sunday School Board. But as the Southern Baptist Convention became more rigid and dogmatic in the 1980s and 1990s, Martin began to wonder if he could in good conscience continue to identify himself as a Southern Baptist.

He quit his job at the Southern Baptist Sunday School Board and accepted the pastorate of a Southern Baptist church in Hawaii. But even there he could not get away from denominational politics. He began to ask himself a difficult question: "Can I stay in this denomination and keep my integrity?" At the time he was still in his 30s and he knew that he could not survive another 30 years in a fundamentalist church. So, he left his pastorate in Hawaii with no job to go to.

Martin and his family returned to Nashville, where they had lived while he was working for the Sunday School Board, and Martin enrolled in a Ph.D. program at Vanderbilt University. As he began his doctoral studies, he also began to look for a new church affiliation. For nine months he studied various denominations and visited various churches. Finally, he narrowed his choices down to three options: Episcopal, Presbyterian, and Methodist. Martin said the Episcopal Church did not need any more clergy at the time, and he couldn't spell Presbyterian, so he went Methodist. All kidding aside, he found in the Methodist church both the biblical foundation and the open-minded faith he had been looking for.

I can relate to that. Frankly, I could see myself feeling at home in the Methodist church except for two things: their practice of infant baptism and their church hierarchy. Martin admits he does not like the Methodist appointment system, where pastors are appointed to a local church by the district superintendent. I'm glad we don't have that appointment system in the Baptist tradition. Each local Baptist church is autonomous and calls its own pastor. Each pastor is responsible to the congregation and not to a district superintendent or bishop. The reason I can remain a Baptist is because of autonomous churches and the biblical foundation and open-minded spirit that characterize our faith.

The latter part of Luke 24 tells how Jesus appeared to a group of his disciples. "They were startled and terrified and thought they were seeing a ghost" (v. 37). Jesus recognized their unbelief and asked, "Why are you frightened, and why do doubts arise in your hearts?" (v. 38). To prove that he was not a ghost, Jesus invited the disciples to touch him. He even ate a piece of broiled fish in their presence. Then he explained how his death and resurrection were the fulfillment of scripture. Finally, he told the disciples to remain together until they would be "clothed with power from on high" (v. 49). In other words, Jesus was preparing them to receive the Holy Spirit. Jesus would not always be present to them in a physical form, but he would be with them in spirit even after they no longer could see him or touch him.

What we have here is really the beginning of the church. Jesus never intended for his followers to go off individually and do their own thing. He told them to stay together and work together and proclaim his name to all nations. We sometimes call it "the Great Commission." Jesus gave his followers a mission, and he expected them to do it together.

Now, I can understand why some people are ready to give up on the church. The church often has failed to carry out the mission of Jesus. Too often, the church has turned the grace of the gospel into a legalistic religion that is intolerant and judgmental. Too often, Christians have been dogmatic and self-righteous and have tried to impose their theology and morality on others. No wonder some sincere seekers are asking, "What is the least I can believe and still be a Christian?"

People want a spiritual connection, but they don't necessarily want all the religious baggage that seems to go along with it. Andrew Sullivan's *Newsweek* story, "Forget the church; [just] follow Jesus," implies that you can follow Jesus apart from the church; that you can be a Christian apart from any organized religion. But that's not what Jesus intended. Jesus told his followers to stay together and wait together to receive power from on high. He told them to work together to proclaim his name throughout the earth.

The truth is that the church has been able to do a lot of good as people have stayed together and worked together to fulfill the mission of Jesus. Yes, there have been injustices committed in the name of religion. But Christians working together have done more good than harm. The mission of the church has reached to healthcare and hospitals, among other things. We could talk about the church's role in the abolition of slavery and the advancement of the Civil Rights Movement. We could talk about the ways that Christians have pushed for prison reform, child welfare laws, hunger relief, peacemaking, protection of the environment, and a host of other social issues. If we give up on organized religion and we each just do our own thing, how can the Christian faith bring any public witness to the critical issues of our time? Plus, if we each just do our own thing, we will miss out on the fellowship and the friendships that so enrich our lives through the church.

I hesitate to tell you what is the least you can believe and still be a Christian, because I don't want to sound legalistic or dogmatic. But for me, the least I can believe and still be a Christian involves two things.

First, I must believe in Jesus. I must believe that he was God's Son, and that he died for my sins, and that he was raised from death for my salvation. I must believe that his life is the example for my life. I don't want to sound judgmental or intolerant, but to believe in Jesus, for me, is fundamental, is essential, to being a Christian.

Second, I must believe in the church. I must believe that Jesus wants me to follow him in community with other believers. People who try to go it alone, those who are not part of a church, will have a hard time living a consistently Christian life. I'm not saying it's impossible. There have been Christian mystics and monks and ascetics who have lived in solitary prayer, largely in isolation from others, but they are the exceptions. For most of us, we need each other. We need the fellowship, support, and nurture of the church. The church is not perfect, but neither is any human organization. But if we stay together and work together and love each other the way that Christ loves us, we can do great things. Our lives will be richer and more blessed in fellowship with one another.

What's the least I can believe and still be a Christian? For me, the least is to believe in Jesus and to believe in the fellowship he created, the community of believers we call the church. Follow Jesus? Yes, of course, absolutely! But forget the church? Absolutely not! The church is the body of Christ, the visible expression of Christ in the world. Christians don't have to be rigid, self-righteous, intolerant, and judgmental. Christians can be like Jesus—kind, compassionate, loving, and filled with grace. That's the kind of church I want to be a part of. That's the kind of Christian I want to be.

MORE THAN A CAMEO
(Luke 24:36-49)

They call it a "cameo." It's a scene in a movie or a television show when a celebrity makes a brief appearance. The film director, Alfred Hitchcock, was famous for his cameos. Hitchcock was a master of suspense, and part of the suspense was guessing where he might pop up in his movies. In *The Birds*, Hitchcock walks past a pet shop with two white terriers. In *North by Northwest*, he misses a bus during the opening credits. In *Rear Window*, he is winding a clock in the neighbor's apartment. In *Dial M for Murder*, he can be seen in a class reunion photo. In *Topaz*, he is pushed through an airport terminal in a wheelchair. It almost became a "Where's Waldo" challenge for movie viewers, trying to spot him, trying to figure out where he would appear next. Alfred Hitchcock's cameo appearances became almost as intriguing as the movies themselves.

The disciples had to be wondering where the risen Jesus would turn up next. He appeared to Mary Magdalene beside the garden tomb (although she had thought he was the gardener). The risen Jesus appeared to a group of women who were making their way back from the empty tomb on Sunday morning. Then he appeared to Simon Peter on the day of the Resurrection, although we don't know all the details of that encounter. Then the risen Jesus appeared to two disciples on the road to Emmaus, although they had presumed he was just another traveler. Then, Jesus appeared to a gathering of disciples in Jerusalem on the evening of the Resurrection.

Among the group were the two from Emmaus, who had returned from Jerusalem to tell about their encounter with the risen Jesus, and "the eleven and their companions." Perhaps some of the women were there too, the ones who had first reported the empty tomb. The room was buzzing with excitement and amazement that Sunday evening. With all these eyewitness accounts, you would think there would have been no doubt that Jesus was alive. But when Jesus suddenly appeared among them, they were "startled and terrified." They thought they were seeing a ghost. Jesus asked them, "Why are you frightened, and why do doubts arise in your hearts?"

This was a good question. In almost all the Resurrection stories, there is some degree of fear and doubt and disbelief. In Luke, the women return from the tomb with the news that Jesus has been raised from the dead, the male disciples do not believe them. They dismiss the account as nonsense, an idle tale. In Matthew 28 we read: "Now the eleven disciples went to Galilee, to the mountain to which Jesus had directed them. When they saw him, they worshipped him; but some doubted" (vv. 16-17). In John 20, Jesus appears to the disciples, but for some reason Thomas is not there. The other disciples tell Thomas, "We have seen the Lord," but Thomas responds, "Unless I see the marks of the nails in his hands, and put my…hand in his side, I will not believe" (v. 25). In Mark's account of the Resurrection, the women flee from the empty tomb in terror and amazement. So, in almost every resurrection story there is a reaction of fear and doubt and disbelief.

The Resurrection is not easy to believe. Some of us have a skeptical bent of mind. Some of us wonder how it was possible for Jesus to rise from the dead. Many of the disciples wondered about it too. Even when some of them told how they had met the risen Jesus face to face, others had a hard time believing it was true. I have never seen anyone arise from the grave. Have you? Yet, the older I get, the more I must confess there are many mysteries in life that I do not fully understand.

When our son Marc was living in New York City, his job entailed a fair amount of travel. It was not unusual for Marc to call us from someplace else. He might call from Boston, from Denver, from Chicago, from Seattle, from Miami, from L.A., from wherever his job would take him. Usually, he would call when he was stuck in traffic or had nothing better to do. We always enjoyed hearing from him, wherever he was calling from. And it really was not much of a novelty to think of him calling from some far-flung location. With the advent of cell phones, people can call from most anywhere. And with our cell phones, Marc could reach us almost anywhere we might be—in the car, at a restaurant, or even in a place far from home. We did not have to know where he was, and he did not have to know where we were in order to reach us.

The risen Jesus had the ability to reach people wherever they were. In the garden outside the tomb, on the road to Emmaus, in the upper room in Jerusalem, on a mountain in Galilee—the risen Jesus was there. Again and again, he appeared to those who loved him, and he answered their fears and doubts with the only thing that mattered—himself. And so, the risen Jesus meets us on the highways and byways of life if we are open to his presence and believe he is here. He comes to us, not as a ghost, but as an unseen spirit, to lift our hearts to hope and to fill us with his love. For two thousand years, people of faith have believed that the risen Christ is here. That does not necessarily eliminate all our doubts, but it gives us something greater than doubts. We have the spiritual presence of our risen Lord.

There is another common thread in almost every resurrection story: Jesus gives his followers something to do. In almost every instance he commissions them to go and tell the good news. In Matthew 28, Jesus commands them to "Go therefore and make disciples of all peoples." In Mark 16, he instructs them to "Go into all the world." In John 20, Jesus teaches: "As the Father has sent me, so I send you." In Acts 1, Jesus issues the charge, "You will be my witnesses." And in Luke 24, he tells them to proclaim repentance and the forgiveness of sins in his name.

Just about every time the risen Jesus appeared to those who loved him, he told them to go out and tell about it: Tell about the Resurrection. Tell about the salvation he offers. Tell about the forgiveness that is available to all who come to him. Tell about the life eternal that is promised to all who follow him. It is not enough to believe that the risen Christ is with us. We are commissioned to share the good news.

I read about a guy in California who spent 30 years collecting pennies. He made a bet with his brother that he could collect a million pennies. It took him three decades, but he finally reached his goal. He collected a million pennies, contained in 20,000 rolls, filling 13 large boxes in his garage. So, he had $10,000 worth of pennies for all his efforts. That was the good news. The bad news was that he had a hard time getting rid of all those pennies. He could not find anyone who would come and haul away 3.5 tons of copper coins without it costing him. His bank would take the pennies for a fee, but it would not take them all at once. One branch offered to take 200 rolls per week. At that rate, it would have taken him nearly two years to cash them all in. The Federal government was not interested in getting involved. A spokesperson for the mint said, "We don't buy back currency. We like to have it in circulation." Here was the real kicker: His brother did not remember they even made a bet 30 years before. So, the penny collector was stuck trying to figure out what to do with all those coins.[4]

Of course, the pennies were still worth something, but that's not what pennies are for. It does not do any good to have 3.5 tons of pennies sitting in a garage. Things of value are not meant to be hoarded. The same is true with our Christian faith. The treasure of a personal relationship with Jesus Christ is not something we are meant to hoard, to keep to ourselves. The gift of salvation, the offer of new life in Christ, is meant to be shared. As the poem says, "love wasn't put in the heart to stay; love isn't love 'til we give it away." So, the risen Jesus has given us something to do.

Alfred Hitchcock made cameo appearances in many of his movies, but his real role was behind the scenes as the director of those movies. Jesus was raised to do more than make cameo appearances now and then. His real role is to direct our lives every day. The risen Christ is here, not just to make us feel good, but to empower us to do good, to witness to and serve others in his name.

WHAT'S NEXT?
(Luke 24:36-49)

When I pastor of Village Baptist Church, in the spring of every year we would recognize the students in our church who were graduating from high school. I would tell them it's a big milestone, a significant achievement, but it's not the end of the story. The real question is: What's next? Will it be college, employment, military service, or some other field of endeavor?

What's next? It is a question that is pertinent not just at graduation, but at many junctures of our lives. Whenever I would counsel a couple about getting married, I would caution them not to devote all their energies during their engagement to planning the wedding. I told them that their wedding was important, of course, but their wedding would be over in a day, while their marriage was meant for a lifetime. The question after the wedding day is: What's next? I can remember talking with some church members who were nearing retirement. Looking toward retirement can be a time filled with both anticipation and apprehension. The question is: what's next?

It was the evening after the Resurrection, and the disciples were asking themselves the same question: What's next? They had heard that Jesus had risen from the dead. Peter had met the risen Jesus, and two other followers were on the way to Emmaus when Jesus appeared to them and stopped to have dinner with them. Some women had met the risen Jesus as they returned from the empty tomb. But the other disciples had not yet had a personal encounter with the risen Christ, and they were still trying to take it all in. They wanted to believe it was true, but the whole idea of Jesus being alive was still too incredible for them to understand.

They were together in Jerusalem talking about the reports of the Resurrection when Jesus appeared among them. Even though they had heard that Jesus was alive, they were startled and filled with fear. They thought they were seeing a ghost. They thought this was some disembodied spirit, some frightening apparition. Jesus recognized that they were afraid and that their hearts were filled with doubts. To calm their fears and assuage their disbelief, he said, "Look at me. See my hands and my feet. [I am the same Jesus who was crucified.] Touch me."

Psychologists tell us that touch is vital to human relationships. People who love each other touch each other. That is why it is customary in our society for people to touch each other when they meet, to greet each other with a handshake or an embrace. In other societies people greet one another with a kiss on the cheek, or a kiss on both cheeks.

Athletes will give each other a high five or a hug after making a good play. Sometimes teams will huddle together and drape their arms on one another's shoulders. For babies, touch is crucial to their development. Babies need a lot of touching. For infants, it is primarily through the experience of touch that they know their parents love them. Before they can understand words or derive meaning from facial expressions, infants learn that they are loved by being touched. Hugs, caresses, kisses, pats, strokes, and other gentle touches help babies to feel safe and secure, to feel a sense of well-being in an otherwise fearful and foreboding world.

When Jesus invited his disciples to touch him, he was communicating with them in the most personal way possible. He was demonstrating that he was alive, but even more, he was assuring them of his love. When Jesus said, "Touch me," it was as if Jesus were saying, "In this fearful and foreboding world, you are safe and secure with me." And then, to show them that they really could believe their eyes and sense of touch, Jesus took a piece of fish and ate it in their presence. He really was alive!

What's next? That is the question. Jesus is alive. Jesus loves us. Jesus has forgiven our sins through his death on the cross. What's next? Unfortunately, many Christians never get around to asking themselves that question: the story stops right here, with Jesus risen from the dead. It's a great moment, but it's not the end of the story. No, the story continues, for Jesus gave his disciples a job to do, and Jesus has given us a job to do. We are to continue what Jesus began, to carry out his message and to carry on his ministry in our world today.

I remember reading a disturbing story in the *Washington Post* some years ago. On a Tuesday morning, at about 6:00 a.m., a truck was involved in an accident on I-395 in Virginia. Traffic had slowed unexpectedly, and the driver of the truck swerved, lost control of his vehicle, hit a guardrail, and overturned. A passenger in the truck, a 36-year-old woman, was thrown from the truck onto the highway. Traffic came to a halt. Drivers began honking their horns and yelling out the windows of their cars, angry that they were being delayed on their way to work. All the while the woman lay on the pavement with severe head injuries. Incredibly, some drivers began to pull their cars onto the shoulder of the road to drive around the debris from the accident and the woman lying on the roadway.

An Army major on his way to work at the Pentagon got out of his vehicle and went over to help the woman. For five minutes, he pleaded with passers-by to use their cell phones to call for help. Most just drove around them. Finally, a civilian computer specialist who worked for the Air Force stopped and called for help. He joined the major standing over the injured woman to prevent passing cars from hitting her. Virginia State Police spokeswoman Lucy Caldwell said, "People didn't stop. They were trying to go around the debris, and they treated her like she was just another piece." Some of the drivers yelled at the Army major and the computer specialist as they passed by, using foul language and obscene gestures, berating them for tying up traffic. The major and the other man stayed with the woman until medical help and the police finally arrived. The woman was taken to Washington Hospital Center where she was admitted in critical condition. Of the major who first stopped to help, the Virginia Police spokeswoman said,

"It was a courageous thing to do. He knew the right thing to do, and some other folks were just in too much of a hurry. Unfortunately, that's more common in this area."[5]

An editorial appeared in the same edition of the *Washington Post* titled, "Hearts of Stone on I-395." The editorial decried the "callousness and blurred moral vision" of those motorists who were more concerned about getting to work on time than they were about helping the woman who lay gravely injured on the road. The *Post* labeled what those drivers did as "heartless and a flagrant transgression against the values of a moral society."

Sadly, we live in a culture where the spirit of the age often seems to be "everyone for himself or herself." After I read the account of the accident just described, I wondered how many of those impatient drivers considered themselves to be Christians. It's all too easy to leave your religion at the door when you leave church on Sunday and rejoin the rat race on Monday. It's all too easy to get caught up in the road rage of traffic congestion and forget about compassion. But if the resurrection of Jesus does not have an impact on the way we live, then we have not understood its meaning. Believing that Jesus died on the cross to save us from our sins is all well and good. Believing that Jesus rose from the grave to give us victory over death is a vitally important part of the message of Easter. But it is all meaningless if it does not make a difference in the way we live.

After Jesus was raised from the dead, he appeared to his disciples not only to show them that he was alive, but also to show them what's next, namely, to tell them he had a job for them to do. They were not just to stay there in the upper room basking in the glow of the Resurrection. They were to go back into the world to continue the work he had begun–the work of sharing God's message, forgiveness, and love with the world.

Of course, being with Jesus and with other believers is wonderful. It must have been wonderful for the disciples to be with the risen Christ that evening after the Resurrection. For us as Christians, we cherish the experience of being with the risen Christ. We cherish going to church, being with other believers, studying the scriptures together, worshipping together. But as good as all that is, there is more to following Jesus. It also involves going out into the world and doing the work that Jesus has called us to do. It involves putting our faith into action. It involves proclaiming the good news about the forgiveness of sins and the gift of eternal life. It involves being moral, ethical, and honest in all the avenues of our lives. It involves ministering to the hurting and the downtrodden with acts of compassion. It involves stopping in the middle of the road, in the middle of our busy schedules, to help someone who has fallen.

The Army major who stopped to render aid to that accident victim said he did it because "it was the right, the Christian thing to do." He did it because he is a follower of Jesus Christ, because that is what a Christian should do. Life is a hectic business for most of us. The danger is that we will pass by people who need our help because we are in too much of a hurry. When it comes to people who need our help, I'm talking about more than accident victims. Anyone who does not have a personal relationship with Jesus, anyone who does not have a church home, that's a person who needs our help. Anyone who does not know that God cares for them, and that other people care about them, that's a person who needs our help. We are to continue what Jesus began. We can do it because by faith we can receive power from on high. That is "what's next."

QUESTIONS FOR DISCUSSION/REFLECTION

1. The risen Jesus could appear and disappear, and yet he could be touched and he could eat. How do you explain this?
2. In what sense has Jesus "appeared" to you?
3. What mission has Jesus given you?
4. In what sense have you "been clothed with power from on high"?
5. Where do you see Jesus in the Old Testament, for example, in the Law of Moses, the Prophets, and the Psalms?

NOTES

[1] *Time*, March 12, 2012.
[2] Reported by Pew Research Center, 2019.
[3] *Newsweek*, April 9, 2012.
[4] *Capital Baptist News Briefs*, April 2006.
[5] *The Washington Post*, April 22, 1998.

CHAPTER 7

THE FIRST DAY
(John 20:1-10)

Early on the first day of the week, while it was still dark, Mary Magdalene came to the tomb and saw that the stone had been removed from the tomb. So she ran and went to Simon Peter and the other disciple, the one whom Jesus loved, and said to them, "They have taken the Lord out of the tomb, and we do not know where they have laid him."
(John 20:1-2 NRSV)

Mary Magdalene was among the women who went to the tomb early on Sunday morning. Matthew, Mark, and John explicitly say she was there, and Luke says it was the women who had followed Jesus from Galilee, which surely would have included Mary Magdalene. In John, the focus is on Mary, although other women must have been with her, for she said, "They have taken the Lord out of the tomb, and we do not know where they have laid him."

After seeing that the stone had been removed from the entrance to the tomb, Mary Magdalene could only conclude that someone had removed Jesus' body. She ran to give the disturbing news to Simon Peter and the disciple whom Jesus loved, presumably John. The two of them took off for the tomb to see for themselves. John, the faster runner, got there first, but only looked inside. He saw the burial wrappings but no body. Peter arrived and went into the tomb to find the wrappings and the cloth that had covered Jesus' head, but again, no body. Then John also entered the tomb and believed, not that Jesus was alive, but that the body was gone. As yet, neither of them understood that Jesus had been raised from the dead. They returned to their homes, trying to process what it all meant.

THE TOMB IS EMPTY
(John 20:1-10)

I was driving east on Central Avenue in Bowie, Maryland, on my way to visit a homebound church member in Edgewater, Maryland. As I neared the bridge that crosses the Patuxent River from Prince George's County into Anne Arundel County, I noticed a large object lying on the side of the road. I slowed down to see what it was. The large object was a deer, which apparently had been struck by a passing car. The animal was not moving, so I assumed it was dead. I did not think much about it at first. The deer population in the area is so large that it not so unusual for one to be hit on the road. But as I continued, I began to think more about it.

I wondered about damage to the vehicle that struck the deer. I wondered whether the collision caused a crash, and whether the driver was injured. I wondered if the driver's insurance rates would go up if a claim were filed. I wondered if someone had notified the city or the county to come and remove the carcass from the side of the road. I wondered if a food pantry could use the meat from the deer, or if it had been dead too long to be edible.

It's amazing how the mind will wander while you're driving. Then I changed the channel on the radio and began to think about other things. By the time I reached the house in Edgewater, I had pretty much forgotten all about the deer.

Looking back, I guess it's too bad a deer was killed on Central Avenue, but I can't say I lost any sleep over it. My reaction would have been quite different that day, however, if I had seen a person lying by the side of the road. I would have stopped immediately and called 911. I would have gone over to see if there was anything I could do to help. If it had been a person lying on the side of the road, I would have been really upset.

A few years ago, when I heard about a little girl and her grandmother who were hit crossing the street on Route 197 in Bowie, I could not stop thinking about it. I drive past that location all the time. It's right across from one of my favorite restaurants. I travel that way to get my hair cut and to go to the Bowie golf course. I know that intersection well, at Route 197 and Old Chapel Road.

When I heard about the little girl and her grandmother, it touched me deeply, even though I did not know them. The 2-year old, Dynesti Hope Maraj, was killed, and her grandmother was hospitalized with serious but non-life-threatening injuries. It was a terrible, tragic accident, and the whole community shared in the grief of the family. When a deer dies, we hardly take notice. But when a person dies, it's a whole different thing.

When Jesus died on the cross, it was a devastating loss for his family and friends. Because the Sabbath was fast approaching, two prominent community leaders, Joseph of Arimathea and Nicodemus, gave Jesus' body a hasty burial before sunset. But early on Sunday morning, while it was still dark, Mary Magdalene and some other women went to the tomb. They intended to complete the burial rituals and to begin the process of formal mourning. They were shocked, however, to see that the large stone that had sealed the entrance to the tomb was removed.

The only conclusion that Mary could imagine was that someone had stolen the body. So, she ran to tell Simon Peter and the other disciple, presumably John, who wrote this account. Mary said, "They have taken the Lord out of the tomb, and we do not know where they have laid him." All of them were already grief-stricken because Jesus had been crucified. For someone they loved to die in such a horrible and agonizing manner was beyond tragic. Now their grief was compounded by the fear that someone had stolen his body out of the grave.

Peter and John took off to see for themselves. There were a lot of reasons for them not to take Mary at her word:

- Mary was a woman, and the testimony of a woman was considered inferior to that of a man.
- Mary was a sole witness giving the report. Typically, two or more witnesses were required to verify authenticity.
- Mary was from Magdala, a town in Galilee with such a poor reputation that the rabbis later attributed its fall to wickedness.
- Mary had a history of mental instability. In Luke's Gospel, we read that Mary had been cured of evil spirits and that seven demons had gone out of her. Anyone with that kind of background might have their sanity questioned.

So, there were reasons for Peter and John to doubt Mary and to run to the tomb to see for themselves. The two started out together, but John, the younger, ran faster and arrived at the tomb first. He bent down and looked inside the burial cave and saw the linen wrappings lying there. But he was hesitant to go inside. When Peter arrived, he did not hesitate. Peter rushed into the tomb and saw the linen wrappings and also the cloth that had been used to cover Jesus' face, neatly rolled up and set aside by itself. This scene did not look like the work of grave robbers. Everything was too orderly, almost serene. Grave robbers would not have left behind the expensive linen wrappings. They would not have left things in such order.

When John went inside the burial chamber, he saw what Peter saw and John "believed." Did John believe that Jesus had been raised from the dead, or did John simply believe that what Mary had said was true, that the tomb was empty? My guess is that both Peter and John did not fully understand what had happened, "for as yet they did not understand the scripture that he must rise from the dead" (John 20:9). So, they left the empty tomb and returned to their homes.

Unlike Mary and Peter and John, we know what happened. We know why the tomb was empty. We know because we have the benefit of the Bible and 20 centuries of Christian history. We know that the tomb was empty, not because someone had stolen the body, but because Jesus had been raised from the dead. Soon, Mary and Peter and John and the other disciples would know that too. Soon, the risen Jesus would appear to all of them. But unlike them, we don't have the benefit of having seen the risen Jesus face to face. Even if he did appear today, how would we recognize him?

None of us knew Jesus in the flesh. All we have are our own imaginations of what he might have looked like. And even those who had known him in his risen form—at least, not at first. The Resurrection was so good, they had a hard time believing it was true. But eventually, these followers of Jesus did believe that he had been raised from the dead, and eventually their mourning turned to joy.

The Resurrection meant that their martyred Master was now their living Lord. The tragedy of his crucifixion had turned into the triumph of his resurrection. It meant that Jesus is alive forevermore, that love is more powerful than hate, that God's power is greater than evil, that the light shines in the darkness and the darkness cannot overcome it, that life is stronger than death. What does the resurrection of Jesus mean for us?

At the age of 10, in June of 1962, I had just finished 5th grade. I was eligible to move from Cub Scouts to Boy Scouts. To mark that transition, members of my Cub Scout pack were invited to join the Boy Scouts for a several-night camping trip to Possum Kingdom Lake, about 110 miles west of my home in Fort Worth, Texas.

One of the members of our pack was another 10-year-old boy named Tommy. He was different from the rest of the boys because he was an epileptic. I vividly remember one day at school when Tommy had a seizure and fell from his desk. We watched in horror as he convulsed on the floor while the teacher tried to keep him from swallowing his tongue. Medications to control epileptic seizures were not as effective then as they are today, so it was a terrifying experience to see a classmate experience something like that. But even though Tommy had epilepsy, still he was allowed to be a part of our scout group, and he went camping with us that week.

On the second day of our camping trip, we went swimming in the lake. Tommy was not supposed to go into the water because of his epilepsy, but he went in anyway. It was only later that the counselors started looking for Tommy around the campsite. No one had seen him. It was getting dark, and our scout leader gathered us around the campfire and tried to keep us distracted by having us sing. Off in the distance down by the lake I could see figures silhouetted by the glow of lanterns. No one told us what was going on, but I later learned they had pulled Tommy from the water and were trying to revive him. The next morning the scout master came to each tent and gently told us that Tommy had died. Our camping trip was over, and our parents were coming to take us home. It was a sad day I will never forget.

Even at age 10, that was not my first experience with death. My grandfather had died when I was 7 years old. But Tommy was my age, and if he could die, that meant that I could die too. Sooner or later, all of us must confront the inevitability of our mortality. Sooner or later, we realize that life on earth will come to an end. What then?

The resurrection of Jesus does not eliminate all the tragedies of life; it transforms them. I still remember Tommy, and I still think about Dynesti. Their deaths were tragic, and their families grieved. Their loss will never be forgotten. But death is not the final word. Life is stronger than death. When I heard Dynesti's full name, I wondered if it were a cruel joke: Dynesti Hope Maraj. Is "hope" just a "mirage" in the face of such unspeakable loss? No, "for neither death…nor anything else in all creation will be able to separate us from the love of God in Christ Jesus our Lord" (Rom. 8:38-39).

On March 14, 2020, Dynesti's mother wrote this obituary for *The Washington Post*:

DYNESTI HOPE LAZINA MARAJ

Our family chain is broken and nothing seems the same, but as God calls us one by one, the chain will link again. Those we love don't go away; they walk beside us every day unseen, unheard but always near. Still loved, still missed and very dear. An angel in the Book of Life wrote down my baby's birth July 7, 2012 and whispered as she closed the book "Too beautiful for Earth." Heaven was blessed on March 14, 2015.

The tomb is empty. Our hearts are full. The loving arms of God will never let us go.

BY DAWN'S EARLY LIGHT
(John 20:1-10)

The plane took off just after 6:00 p.m. Our destination was Phoenix, Arizona, for a few days of sunshine and golf. As I looked out the window of the aircraft, I saw the sun was setting just ahead of us. There was a luminous glow all along the horizon where the clouds met the sky. Because we were flying due west, it took a long time for the sun to set. I watched it off and on for about an hour until the sky finally turned black. I knew the night was coming, but for a while the setting sun almost stood still. Finally, darkness overcame the light. It was the proverbial "long day's journey into night."

That must have been how the disciples felt when Jesus died—a long day's journey into night. When Jesus was nailed to the cross, they knew the night was coming. He had saved others, but he would not save himself. It was only a matter of time until the darkness descended and Jesus died. Because the Sabbath, which began at sundown, was fast approaching, there was not time to properly prepare his body for burial. So, his body was hastily carried to a rock-hewn tomb and laid to rest in a burial cave with a large stone sealing shut the door.

The light returned the next morning, on Saturday, the Jewish Sabbath, but all day long it must have seemed like it was still night. Jesus was dead and buried, and with him the hopes and dreams of those who loved him. It must have been the most mournful Sabbath ever. Then early the next morning, on Sunday, the first day of the week, well before dawn, while it was still dark, Mary Magdalene led a sorrowful group of women to the place where Jesus had been laid.

Then, by dawn's early light, Mary saw to her astonishment and anguish that the stone had been rolled away from the entrance to the tomb. She ran to tell Simon Peter and the disciple whom Jesus loved. With a mixture of shock and horror and sorrow, she breathlessly blurted out: "They have taken the Lord out of the tomb, and we don't know where they have laid him!" In Mary's mind, it was a worst-case scenario: Not only was Jesus dead, but his body was missing—either stolen by grave robbers or desecrated by those who had killed him.

Grave robbery was all too common in those days when many tombs were above ground in natural or man-made caves. Because burial customs often included expensive, linen grave clothes and costly spices for anointing, there was a financial incentive for those who chose to break into tombs. John tells us in chapter 19 that even though Jesus had been hastily buried, an affluent benefactor named Nicodemus had wrapped the body in linen cloths along with a hundred pounds of myrrh and aloes, a burial fit for a king. Such a burial, in a new rock-hewn tomb where no one had been laid before, would have been a tempting target for robbers.

For Mary, the sight of the empty tomb was anything but good news. Seeing the stone rolled away sent a shiver of dread through her body. For Mary, it was a further indignity heaped upon the horrible memory forever seared in her mind of Jesus dying in agony on the cross. Could things get any worse, Mary must have thought to herself. Not only had Jesus died the vilest of deaths, but now his body was missing.

Peter and the Beloved Disciple, presumably John, sprinted for the tomb to see for themselves. John, perhaps the younger of the two, ran faster and reached the tomb first, but he hesitated to go inside until Peter arrived. Instead, John stood outside the tomb and bent down to look through the low doorway into the burial chamber, illumined only by the rays of the rising sun. He saw the linen wrappings lying there, but no body.

Then Peter arrived and, true to his impulsive nature, went straightway inside the grave. He too saw the linen wrapping lying there, and the cloth that had been placed over Jesus' head. It did not make any sense. What robbers would steal the body but leave the valuable grave clothes behind?

John joined Peter inside the burial chamber. Seeing the grave clothes lying there, John believed what Mary Magdalene had said: the body of Jesus was gone. At that moment, John and Peter did not fully understand the scripture, that Jesus would rise from the dead.

Even for us today, there are things about the resurrection of Jesus that we do not fully understand. How could a dead man come back to life? How could a body that had lain in the grave for three days be raised to new life? How could Jesus break the bonds of death and leave his grave clothes behind?

There was no sign of struggle, unlike the resuscitated Lazarus who had emerged from the tomb still bound. The grave clothes were lying in the tomb not in disarray, not scattered on the floor, not in a disheveled heap, but lying there as if Jesus' body had somehow evaporated out of them. The resurrected Jesus did not struggle to remove the wrappings; he did not take off the linen bindings. It was as if his body had dematerialized, leaving the grave clothes as they were. We do not understand how Jesus was resurrected from the dead, but then there are a lot of things we do not understand.

Some years ago, my church purchased a new Internet service for the computers in our offices. The wireless DSL router was installed in another part of the building. A tiny receiver and transmitter would receive and send signals invisibly through the air. I did not understand exactly how it worked, but when I would send an email, the signal would leave my office and fly through the air to the router in the office down the hall. Then the message would somehow end up on the computer of the person I sent the email to, even if that computer were halfway around the world. One day my curiosity got the better of me, and I tried to physically block the transmission of the wireless signals. I stood between the transmitter in my office and the router down the hall, but the transmission still went through. Maybe the radio waves passed right through my body, but I did not feel a thing.

There are all kinds of mysteries in modern technology that I do not understand, and that would have seemed impossible to people of previous generations. When my grandparents were born, who could have imagined electricity, automobiles, airplane travel, rockets to the moon, air conditioning, and all the marvels of modern medicine? Machines that can look inside your body—x-rays, MRIs, CT scans? Laser eye surgery that can correct near-sightedness in a few painless moments? Vaccines and antibiotics and other miracle drugs that can prevent or cure formerly fatal diseases? There is a lot that I cannot explain or fully understand.

The First Day

I cannot explain how Jesus was resurrected from the dead. I cannot explain how his body passed through his grave clothes into a resurrected state. Someday maybe our minds will understand how it could have happened, but for now we are like those first disciples who did not fully understand and yet who came to believe. We have not seen the grave clothes lying in the tomb, but we have seen other evidence that Jesus was raised from the dead. The very existence of the church and the Christian faith is powerful evidence that Jesus is alive. In the lives of changed people we see compelling evidence of the presence of the risen Christ. Most compellingly, I have felt the presence of the risen Christ in my own life. As the old hymn says, "You ask me how I know he lives? He lives within my heart!"

Something happened the Sunday morning after Jesus' crucifixion that we do not fully understand, but that has changed the world. For 20 centuries the followers of Jesus have believed that the Cross was not the end, the grave was not final, and death was not the victor. We join countless saints through the ages as we proclaim that Jesus is alive. He slipped the surly bonds of death and rose to new and eternal life. He left his grave clothes behind and assumed a spiritual body not confined to the limitations of Earth. Because Jesus lives, our long day's journey into night has become a long night's journey into day.

Jesus said, "No one has greater love than this, to lay down one's life for one's friends" (John 15:13). That is what Jesus did: He laid down his life for us all and then rose from the grave to give new life to all who believe in him. This is the good news: The light shines in the darkness, and the darkness has never overcome it. The grave was empty because Jesus is alive. And, whoever believes in him will not perish but will receive eternal life.

24 HOURS OF HOPE
(John 20:1-10)

She worked long hours at minimum wage. Even with overtime pay, she could barely make ends meet for herself and her kids. The father of her children was long gone, and her parents were not around to help. So, she struggled alone. It might sound foolish, but out of her meager earnings she bought a lottery ticket every week. A friend asked her why she was willing to part with her hard-earned money that way. The woman replied, "It's not too much to pay for 24 hours of hope."

Now, I am not a fan of the lottery or other forms of gambling. For every lottery winner, there are millions of losers. Gambling is addictive for some people, and whatever good the proceeds from gambling might accomplish, it hardly makes up for the cost in ruined lives. Yet, I can understand the woman's rationale. A few dollars spent does not seem too much to pay for 24 hours of hope. The only trouble is, it's a hope that does not last. After 24 hours, the hope is gone.

It seemed as if hope was gone for the disciples. On Thursday night Jesus had gathered with them in an upper room in Jerusalem to share the Passover together. Less than 24 hours later, Jesus was dead and buried, the disciples were hiding like frightened animals, and it seemed like all hope was lost.

When Mary Magdalene made her way to the tomb early on Sunday morning, she was without hope too. She had seen Jesus die, and she had seen his lifeless body placed in the tomb. When Mary saw that the stone was rolled away from the entrance to the tomb, she was distraught. She assumed it was the work of grave robbers. That's why she ran to tell Peter and John. In a panic, the two disciples took off for the tomb at break-neck speed. John reached the tomb first and stopped at the entrance to look inside. He saw the grave clothes lying there, but no body, no corpse. Peter arrived, and without hesitation, charged into the burial cave, also finding it empty. The disciples knew at that moment that Jesus was no longer there, but they did not yet understand that he had risen from the dead.

In her book, *The Complete Book of Death and Dying*, Constance Jones describes the burial practices of the prehistoric Neanderthals. Jones writes that the Neanderthals would often bury their dead with the remains of a bear. Why a bear, we might ask. Because those primitives knew that bears hibernate in the winter and emerge from their caves in the spring. To the Neanderthals, the bear was a symbol of death and rebirth. They imagined that if they would bury their dead with a bear, there might be some hope for life beyond the grave. Humankind has always sought some reassurance that life does not end at death.

A man was known to be a Christian. He did not wear his religion on his sleeve, but his co-workers knew that he was a man of faith. Most of them respected his beliefs, but one fellow employee was cynical and hostile. He said with a contemptuous tone of voice, "You Christians think you are better than anyone else, don't you?" The man replied, "No, we're not better; we're only better off."

We Christians are not better than anyone else. We have problems, we make mistakes, and we suffer from the trials and tribulations of life in this world. We are sinners like everyone else, in need of forgiveness. We're not better, but we are better off. We are better off because we have a Savior. We are better off because Jesus died for our sins and then rose from the grave to give us eternal life. We are better off because the Holy Spirit is with us to give us peace.

Andrew Meekens was on the Ethiopian Airlines flight that was hijacked over the Indian Ocean in November of 1996. Hijackers ordered the pilot to fly to a destination that was beyond the plane's range. Eventually the plane ran out of fuel, and the pilot announced to the passengers that he would have to attempt an emergency landing in the ocean. Needless to say, the passengers became frantic. Meekens, an elder in the International Evangelical Church in Addis Ababa, stood up and began to calm the other passengers. He told them that they were in God's hands, and then he shared with them about his faith in Jesus. A flight attendant who survived the crash landing said that about 20 people, including another flight attendant who died in the crash, responded to Meekens' testimony and asked Christ into their hearts. Meekens was among those killed in the crash, but he never lost hope. Even now his family is comforted by the hope that he is at rest and at peace with his Father in heaven.

We who believe in Jesus have 24 hours of hope. But unlike the hope of winning the lottery, which vanishes after every drawing, our 24 hours of hope never end. We who believe in Jesus have won the lottery of life. We have 24 hours of hope every day, because Jesus, our Savior, lives.

QUESTIONS FOR DISCUSSION/REFLECTION

1. When When Mary Magdalene saw that the stone had been removed from the tomb, it never occurred to her that Jesus had been raised from the dead. What would your reaction have been?
2. What was the meaning of the linen wrappings lying in Jesus' tomb? Of the cloth that had been on Jesus' head rolled up in a place by itself?
3. The disciple who reached the tomb first went in, "and he saw and believed." What did he see, and what did he believe?
4. John wrote, "as yet they did not understand the scripture, that he must rise from the dead." To what scripture was John referring?

CHAPTER 8

JESUS APPEARS TO MARY
(John 20:11-18)

> *As soon as she had said this, she turned around and saw Jesus standing there, but she didn't know it was Jesus. Jesus said to her, "Mary." Mary Magdalene left and announced to the disciples, "I've seen the Lord." (John 20:14, 16a, 18a CEB)*

Mary was crying. Standing outside the tomb she was bereft that someone had taken away the body of Jesus. Through her tears she looked in the tomb and saw two angels where Jesus had been laid. They asked her why she was crying. She blurted out, "They have taken away my Lord." Then she turned around and saw Jesus standing there, but did not recognize him. He asked her why she was crying. Mary thought he was the caretaker of the garden where the tomb was located. Then Jesus called her by name, "Mary," and she knew who he was. She called him, "Rabbouni," which meant Teacher. That's who he was to her—her Teacher, her Lord.

Mary's instinct was to grab hold of Jesus, but Jesus told her not to cling to him. Their relationship could not continue like that because he would not be with her for long in a physical way. Soon he would ascend to his Father and her Father, his God and her God. Instead of holding on to him, she should go and tell his brothers and sisters about him. By this time, Mary's tears of grief had turned into tears of gladness. She went and announced to the disciples, "I have seen the Lord!" Her sadness had turned to joy.

HE CALLS YOU BY NAME
(John 20:11-18a)

My friend Stanley defines a good restaurant as one with tablecloths and cloth napkins. Linda and I don't dine at that kind of establishment very often. We tend to eat at restaurants where we stand in line to place our order at the register, and then wait for our food at the end of the counter. I've noticed that some of those restaurants will ask for your name instead of giving you a number. I guess they think it's more personal to call out a name instead of a number. I prefer the number. Whenever they ask for my name, I say, "Just give me a number."

There is something personal about a name. I'd rather my name not be used in some impersonal business transaction. Why do they need to know my name? I'm probably never going to see those people again. I'm probably not going to have a meaningful conversation with them or start up a lasting friendship. They're just going to hand me my food, and then move on to the next customer. Linda doesn't like it when they ask for my name and I tell them to just give me a number. So, I give them *her* name, but she doesn't like that either. She told me if I don't want to give them my name, just to make up a name to give them.

Most recently, I've been using the name "Jack." Sometimes I give the name "Bob." I apologize to any "Jacks" or "Bobs" for using your name. I selected those pseudonyms because they are both easy to spell. Occasionally, when I am eating out by myself, I will get a little mischievous and give them a more complicated biblical name such as "Bartholomew" or "Melchizedek." Workers at fast food restaurants don't like it when I do that. They give me a dirty look, like, "What, are you nuts?"

When people know your name, they know something very personal about you. I was named after my two grandfathers. My first name pays tribute to my mother's father, Bruce Shulkey. My middle and last names, Campbell Salmon, come from my father's side of the family. Campbell was my father's middle name, and his father's middle name, and his father's middle name, and his mother's maiden name. So, the "Campbell" goes back more than 200 years to my great-great-grandmother, Mary Campbell. We passed the Campbell name on to our son Marc. When Marc Campbell Salmon and his wife Stacey were expecting a baby girl, we suggested that Campbell could be a girl's name. They named her Ford, which was Linda's maiden name.

According to John 20, Mary Magdalene had come to the tomb early on Sunday morning. Her name was Mary, and the Magdalene probably meant that she was from the town of Magdala in Galilee. Back then not everyone had a first, middle, and last name. People were sometimes identified by where they came from, or by who their father was. Mary was a common name in biblical times. Jesus knew at least four women named Mary: his mother Mary; Mary, the mother of Joses; Mary, the sister of Martha and Lazarus; and this Mary, called Magdalene, from whom seven demons had gone out (Luke 8:2). Some of the Marys were there when Jesus died on the cross. At least two of the Marys had come to the tomb while it was still dark on the first day of the week.

When Mary Magdalene saw that the stone had been removed from the tomb, she ran to tell Peter and the beloved disciple, presumably John. They took off to see for themselves. Apparently, Mary followed them back to the tomb. After verifying it was empty, Peter and John returned home. But Mary remained outside the tomb, weeping. She still did not know that Jesus had been raised from the dead. She was weeping because she thought that someone had stolen his body.

As she wept, Mary bent down to look in the tomb. There she saw two angels, where the body of Jesus had lain. They asked her, "Woman, why are you weeping?" Mary said to the angels basically what she had said to Peter and John: "They have taken away my Lord, and I don't know where they have laid him."

Turning away from the angels, Mary saw Jesus standing there in the garden, but she did not know it was Jesus. He asked her, "Woman, why are you weeping? For whom are you looking?" Assuming Jesus would be the gardener, the caretaker of the cemetery, Mary responded: "Sir, if you have carried him away, tell me where you have laid him." Jesus said to her, "Mary!" And immediately she knew who he was. It was only when Mary heard Jesus call her by name that she realized he was alive and had risen from the dead.

There is great power in a name. Generally, when people call us by name, we feel acknowledged, we feel affirmed, and we feel we matter. I suppose that's the premise behind fast food restaurants wanting to call me by name rather than giving me a number. But while I don't feel particularly affirmed by hearing my name called at a food counter, I do feel tremendously affirmed when someone cares about me enough to know my name.

To me, this is one of the most remarkable things about Jesus: he knew people's names. He wasn't just interested in drawing big crowds and becoming famous. He really cared about people on an individual level. And remarkably, many of the people he cared about individually were those on the margins of society. Jesus interacted with all kinds of marginal people—women, Gentiles, Samaritans, children, tax collectors, lepers, the blind, the lame, the sick, the poor, the demon-possessed. Mary was a case in point.

Mary had been a demoniac. People tended to stay away from people who were not in their right minds, but Jesus didn't stay away from her. He cured her of evil spirits, simply because he cared about her. Because Jesus cared about Mary, he knew her name. Jesus was the Son of God, yet he humbled himself and took the form of a servant. No one was beneath his dignity. Yes, Jesus was better than everyone else, but he never acted like it. He treated every person as worthy to be known and affirmed and loved.

One of my favorite stories in the Gospel of John is when Jesus raised Lazarus from the dead (chapter 11). After Lazarus fell ill, his sisters sent a message to Jesus that their brother was sick. No doubt, they wanted Jesus to come and heal him. Even though Jesus loved Lazarus and his sisters, he did not rush to Lazarus' side. Jesus stayed two days longer in the place where he was. When Jesus finally arrived, Lazarus was dead. His body had been in the tomb four days.

After Jesus met with the grieving sisters, he was "greatly disturbed in spirit and deeply moved." As Jesus came to the tomb, the scripture tells us that "Jesus wept." He didn't just shed a tear or two. The Greek word for "wept" literally means he "burst out crying." Jesus sobbed beside the tomb of his friend Lazarus. Why did Jesus weep? He knew what he was going to do. He knew he was going to call Lazarus to come forth from the tomb. I think Jesus wept and was "greatly disturbed in spirit" and was "deeply moved" because he genuinely cared about the sisters of Lazarus, Mary and Martha. He knew they were hurting, and in great empathy, he was hurting too.

To me, this is what separates the Christian faith from every other religion. In most other religions, god is an impersonal, remote deity, distant and detached from human existence. If the god of other religions is involved in human life at all, it's only as a harsh and demanding judge. But Jesus put a human face on God. He represented God in the most deeply personal way. Jesus presented God as a loving heavenly Father who cares for all his children. And because God cares for us, Jesus knows when we are hurting, and when we cry, he cries too. And because God cares for us, he wants us to care for each other too.

I knew the names of most of the people who attended the church I served as pastor—not everyone, but most. If I didn't know their names, that meant they had not introduced themselves to me, or maybe I had forgotten, or maybe they did not want me to know their names. That's okay—people could remain anonymous if they wanted to. But no one is anonymous with God. He knows all our names and everything about us, but he loves us anyway—even though he knows stuff about us we don't want anyone to know.

When the risen Jesus came to Mary in the garden, he called her by name. He did it because he loved her and wanted her to know that he would keep on loving her, no matter what. Nothing, not even death, could separate her from his love. Jesus gave himself for us so we might know of his love. All he wants is for us to love and follow him in return. Listen, listen, listen…He's calling you by name.

SURPRISE AND EXPECTATION
(John 20:11-18a)

My wife Linda says that she is not much of a cook, but she makes a delicious Chinese stir-fry dish. We have it for dinner often. One night, after we had eaten, Linda said she had a surprise for dessert. She opened the pantry and brought out a box of fortune cookies she had bought at the dollar store. (Get this: those Chinese fortune cookies were made in America! That was a real surprise, as everything seems to come from China these days.)

We each took a cookie out of the box and unwrapped the cellophane wrapper. I broke my cookie in half and took out the fortune. It read, "Look to the next month for some pleasant surprises." It also had some numbers printed on the bottom, in case I wanted to play the lottery. Linda broke open her cookie and took out the fortune. It read, "Keep your expectations reasonable." We laughed when we put our two fortunes together. Mine said, "Look to the next month for some pleasant surprises." Hers said, "Keep your expectations reasonable." I guess if we play the numbers in the lottery, we should not expect to win the jackpot.

Those two fortunes represent two ways of looking at life. We all have expectations of what the future may bring, but occasionally there are surprises we did not expect.

Mary Magdalene went to the tomb early on Sunday morning after Jesus' crucifixtion, expecting to find the body of Jesus lying in the grave. She was keeping her expectations reasonable. After all, Mary had seen Jesus die an agonizing death on the cross. She had watched as Joseph of Arimathea and Nicodemus anointed his body with spices, wrapped it in a linen cloth, and laid it in a rock-hewn tomb. Mary knew that Jesus was dead, and she fully expected to find his body in the tomb when she returned early that Sunday morning to complete the rituals of burial.

To her shock and dismay, though, when Mary arrived she saw the stone had been removed from the tomb's entrance. She was not expecting that. It was not a pleasant surprise. Mary concluded that grave robbers had come and stolen the body during the night. She ran to tell Simon Peter and John this shocking and dismaying news. With a mixture of panic and heartbreak, Mary said: "They have taken the Lord out of the tomb, and we do not know where they have laid him."

Peter and John were equally alarmed, and they took off to see for themselves. John outran Peter and arrived at the tomb first. He stopped outside the tomb and bent down

Jesus Appears to Mary

and looked in. There he saw the linen burial wrappings lying on the ground. When Peter arrived, he ran straight into the tomb and saw the linen wrappings and the cloth that had covered Jesus' head rolled up in a place by itself. John then entered the tomb and saw that the body of Jesus was not there. He believed the tomb was empty, but neither Peter nor John yet understood that Jesus had risen from the dead. Still perplexed, the two disciples returned to their homes.

Mary had followed Peter and John back to the tomb, and she stood there weeping. As she wept, she bent over to look inside the tomb. Then she saw two angels, dressed in white, sitting at the head and the foot of the place where the body of Jesus had lain. The angels said to Mary, "Woman, why are you weeping?" She replied, "They have taken away my Lord, and I do not know where they had laid him." Having said this, Mary turned around and saw Jesus standing there, but she did not know it was Jesus. She assumed he was the gardener.

Jesus asked her, "Woman, why are you weeping? Whom are you looking for?" She answered, "Sir, if you have carried him away, tell me where you have laid him, and I will take him away." Jesus called her name, "Mary!" Suddenly she recognized who he was. She said, "Teacher." Jesus told her not to hold on to him, but to go and tell his disciples. Mary went and announced to the disciples, "I have seen the Lord!" It was not what they had been expecting. Rather, it was a surprise that changed everything.

I don't know about you, but my life is more about expectations than surprises. In fact, I generally don't like surprises, because in my experience most surprises are not very good. And as my fortune cookie advised, I try to keep my expectations reasonable. So, I can relate to Mary and the other disciples. No one expected Jesus to rise from the dead, even though he had predicted it. The Resurrection was a complete surprise to everyone. John 20 tells about the great surprise that is Easter. It is the "great surprise" because Easter reformulates all our expectations about life. It gives us a hope that nothing in this world can take away.

In 1982 I returned to The Southern Baptist Theological Seminary for my Doctor of Ministry degree. Unlike the Master of Divinity program when I lived in Louisville and went to school full-time, the Doctor of Ministry program required residency on campus just a month or two a year. The residency requirements were called J-terms, since we were on campus only in January, June, or July. Needless to say, those J-terms were intensive. They required a lot of advance reading, and once we were there, we were in class all day. Some of my classmates went back to their churches on the weekends for Sunday services, but I took vacation time and study leave so I could be in Louisville the entire month for each J-term. Linda and the kids went with me for three J-terms so they could visit with her family while I was in class or studying in the library. One January J-term our daughter Amy even went to an elementary school in Louisville.

One of my professors for a J-term seminar was Frank Tupper, a professor of theology. During that month I came to learn that he and his family were going through a serious health crisis. Frank's wife, Betty, then in her 30s, had been diagnosed with cancer. Frank and Betty had two school-age children. Most days after class Frank would go home to prepare dinner for the kids, then he would go to the hospital to sit with his wife. During that J-term after we became aware of what was going on in Frank's family, our theological discussions in class moved beyond abstract debates. Betty Tupper, wife of our seminary professor, mother of two young children, was fighting for her life. We all felt a sense of anguish. We raised tough questions about the providence of God and the meaning of suffering. There were no simple answers. We knew that there was a young wife lying in a hospital bed with cancer and two children eating dinner at home every night without their mother.

After the J-term was over, my family returned to Maryland. The crisis in the Tupper family was no longer so immediate for us. But I later learned that Betty's illness had failed to respond to medical treatments. As she grew sicker and it became likely that the cancer would end her life, Frank faced an intensely personal theological crisis. As my friend and fellow pastor Terry Lester put it, Frank "entered the abyss where God seemed painfully silent, if not absent. During his crisis Frank Tupper wrote a note to himself saying he wasn't sure if he believed in God any longer."

After Betty died, Frank gave a sermon in the seminary chapel. He described a dream he had during that dark time of Betty's illness. In his dream, Frank was running along a beach at night during a violent thunderstorm. As the surf crashed against the shore, Frank saw a face with a cruel smile appear above the angry waves, and he heard the sound of mocking laughter. Above the face a neon sign flashed off and on like bolts of lightning, with just one word: "Chaos. Chaos, Chaos." For a time, Frank wasn't sure he believed in God anymore, but where else could he turn? Years later Dr. Tupper wrote a book about suffering and the love of God, which he titled *A Scandalous Providence*.

The Resurrection was the great surprise that reformulates our expectations about life. But even though Jesus was raised from the dead, suffering and death are still a part of life. Young mothers still get sick and die, children still lose parents, husbands still lose wives, and personal chaos can lead even a seminary professor into such a dark night of the soul that he wonders if he still believes in God.

During the last stage of Betty Tupper's illness Frank tried stay by her bedside as much as possible, but he could not be there all the time. He had teaching responsibilities at the seminary, and he had children at home who needed him. So, when Frank wasn't there at the hospital, a close friend of the family who was a chaplain at the hospital would often fill in. The chaplain would go into Betty's room and just sit by her bed for long stretches of time. Often there would be very little conversation. The chaplain wouldn't say much, but he would just let Betty know he was there. After Betty died, the chaplain fulfilled her wishes by participating in her funeral. During the funeral, the chaplain was seated on the platform, but he never spoke. Finally, the presiding pastor explained the chaplain's silent presence on the platform. He said the chaplain was there at Betty's request to "represent the silent presence of God."

When Jesus died on the cross, it seemed that God was painfully silent, if not absent. God did not spare his own Son from suffering and death. But on Easter Sunday the silence of God was broken. The earth shook, the stone was rolled away, and Jesus came forth from the tomb alive. It was the great surprise that reformulates all our expectations about life. Suffering and death are real, but they are not the final reality. Because Jesus died for our sins and was raised from the dead by the power of God, we always have hope.

In his book, *The Sacred Canopy*, sociologist Peter Berger wrote that the true test of religion is the "hope it gives people in the face of death." The resurrection of Jesus is our hope in the face of death. It is our hope that we too will be raised to new life. In the end it was the story of Jesus that gave Frank Tupper hope and allowed him to keep his faith in God. In his book, *A Scandalous Providence*, Frank Tupper wrote:

> Of course I cannot speak for anyone else, only for me, but this I know: without the story of Jesus, I would not believe in God. Or more probably, God simply would not matter. The story of Jesus enables me to envision God as one who genuinely cares for each and for all of us. In Jesus, God confronts the darkness face to face, incarnate for our sake. Jesus is the light of the gentle face of God, and the story of Jesus says that God laughs with us in our joys, and weeps with us in our sorrows. God strengthens us in our helplessness. God stands with us in the uncertainty of our believing, and God waits for us in our yearning to belong. Ultimately, it is the lonely companionship of Jesus, the suffering of his Passion, that makes my painful journey a sometime story of faith.

After Frank Tupper left Southern Seminary, he became professor of theology at the Wake Forest University Divinity School where he continued to think and write and teach and preach about suffering and the love of God. In fact, he completed an updated version of his book, *A Scandalous Providence*, which was released in 2013. Sadly, Frank Tupper died in 2020 after a long illness. But the testimony of his life lives on. And every time I think of him, I cannot help but smile.

Linda and I laughed when we broke open our fortune cookies. My fortune read, "Look…for some pleasant surprises." Hers read, "Keep your expectations reasonable." But God got the last laugh when he broke open the tomb and raised Jesus from the dead. Thank God, we are not left to the whims of capricious fortune. Our lives are in the hands of God who loved us so much that he gave us his Son. The great surprise of the Resurrection changes our expectations about life. Now, even in the face of harsh realities, we live in hope. Christ is risen! He is risen indeed!

JESUS IS ALIVE!
(John 20:1-18, 1 Cor. 15:3b-7)

January 18, 1989 was a Wednesday. Don Piper, associate pastor of South Park Baptist Church in Alvin, Texas, was attending a conference sponsored by the Baptist General Convention of Texas. The conference was scheduled to end with lunch that Wednesday, but the final speaker did something Baptist preachers rarely do: he finished early. So, instead of lunch, the staff at the conference center served brunch. Don was on the road shortly after 11:00 a.m. He figured that if the traffic was not too bad, he could make it back to his church by 2 o'clock in the afternoon.

Not long after leaving the conference center, Don reached an old bridge over the Trinity River. Because it was raining and Don was not familiar with the highway, he was driving along at 50 miles an hour in his Ford Escort. Around 11:45 a.m., just before Don reached the east end of the bridge, an 18-wheeler traveling 60 miles an hour approached from the other direction. The truck was driven by an inmate from the Texas Department of Corrections. Suddenly the truck veered across the center line on the bridge and struck Don's vehicle head on. The collision sandwiched Don's car against the bridge railing, and the wheels of the semi rolled on top of Don's car and smashed it. Two prison guards, who were following behind the 18-wheeler in a pickup, called for an ambulance. Within minutes medical help arrived. They examined Don and found that he had sustained massive traumatic injuries. Detecting no pulse, they pronounced him dead at the scene. But that's not the end of the story.

A few minutes later Dick Onerecker, another Baptist pastor who had been at the same conference, happened upon the accident. He felt led to stop his car and see if he could offer assistance. Told by the paramedics that the victim in the Escort was dead, the minister asked if he might say a prayer anyway. Granted permission from the authorities, Rev. Onerecker sat down alongside Don's body and began to pray. After praying for a long time, Rev. Onerecker began to sing the hymn, "What a Friend We Have in Jesus." He was startled when he heard a voice coming from under the tarp, as the "dead man" began to sing along. Rev. Onerecker summoned the paramedics, who initially refused to believe that the dead man had come back to life. But sure enough, Don Piper was alive, just barely, and they took him to the hospital. There he would spend the next 13 months, enduring 34 operations, to recover from his injuries.

Today, Don Piper is still alive. Although he walks with a limp, he travels all over the country telling his story. In 2004 he wrote a book that became a *New York Times* non-fiction bestseller, with as many as 9 million copies sold in paperback print. The title of the book is *90 Minutes in Heaven*. Don says that during the 90 minutes between the time of the accident and the time he came back to life, he died and went to heaven. The book was made into a full-length film in 2015. There are also videos online in which Piper describes his experiences after he died. Of course, skeptics would say that he did not really die, even though the paramedics could find no pulse and pronounced him dead. Skeptics would say that he was near death, but never crossed the threshold completely. But Don believes his death was real, and that his experiences in heaven were real. And those who were there that day with Don on the bridge believe that he died too.

It was a Friday when Jesus died on the cross, nailed there between two thieves. After hanging in agony for more than six hours, he finally succumbed to multiple injuries inflicted by a brutal beating, nails driven through his hands and feet, and a spear thrust into his side. Whether he died from loss of blood or from shock or asphyxia, we do not know. But we do know that Jesus died and was buried in a borrowed tomb. As far as his disciples were concerned, Jesus was dead and gone, and all their hopes were dead and buried with him. But that's not the end of the story.

Because the Sabbath began at sundown on Friday, his friends could not properly prepare his body for burial. But early on Sunday morning, in the half-light of early dawn, Mary Magdalene and some other women approached the tomb to anoint Jesus' body with spices. They were shocked when they saw that the large stone that had blocked the entrance to the tomb was rolled away, and more alarmed that the body of Jesus was gone. Mary ran to tell Simon Peter and the other disciple, probably John, the author of the Fourth Gospel. The two disciples ran to the tomb to see for themselves. John outran Peter and reached the tomb first, but he did not go in. Stooping down, he saw the burial wrappings lying there. Then Peter arrived and rushed into the burial cave. He also saw the linen wrappings and the cloth that had covered Jesus' head. John then entered the tomb and "believed," although neither disciple understood exactly what had happened.

Mary Magdalene had followed Peter and John back to the tomb, and she stood there after they had left, weeping. Looking in the tomb, she saw two angels dressed in white, sitting where the body of Jesus had been laid. The angels said to her, "Woman, why are you weeping?" Mary said, "They have taken away my Lord, and I do not know where they have laid him." Mary still thought Jesus was dead. Then she turned and saw the risen Jesus standing next to her, but she did not know it was Jesus. He asked her, "Woman, why are you weeping? Whom are you looking for?" Assuming that he was the gardener, the caretaker of the cemetery, she said, "Sir, if you have carried him away, tell me where you have laid him." Jesus said to her, "Mary!" She replied, "Rabbouni!" which means Teacher. Mary went and told the disciples, "I have seen the Lord."

About 90 minutes after that traffic accident in Texas, everyone thought Don Piper was dead. No one believed he had come back to life until Dick Onerecker heard him singing from beneath his death shroud. Three days after Jesus died on the cross, everyone thought he was dead. No one believed that Jesus had come back to life until Peter and John saw the empty tomb and Mary met the risen Jesus face to face. Of course, there are skeptics who doubt Don Piper died and went to heaven, even for 90 minutes, just as there are skeptics who doubt the resurrection of Jesus. But that is what makes the Easter story so compelling: no one expected Jesus to rise from the dead. Even his closest friends did not expect it.

A few years ago, the Barna Research Group conducted a nationwide survey about the meaning of Easter. In telephone interviews with a random sample of more than a thousand adults across the continental United States, they asked, "What does Easter mean to you, personally?" Most Americans know that Easter is a religious holiday, but only 42 percent of those surveyed said that the meaning of Easter is the resurrection of Jesus. Among people who regularly go to church, the percentage was higher: 73 percent of evangelical Christians identified Easter as the celebration of the resurrection of Jesus. But for a lot of people, Easter is little more than new clothes and egg hunts and bunny rabbits.

The first Christians understood the meaning of Easter. It would be three or four centuries before they would celebrate Christmas, but the resurrection of Jesus was the centerpiece of their faith from the very beginning. They even changed their day of worship from the Jewish Sabbath (Saturday) to Sunday, to celebrate the resurrection of their Lord. A decade or more before the Gospels were written, Paul wrote to the church in Corinth: "Christ died for our sins, as the scriptures say. He was buried, and three days later he was raised to life" (1 Cor. 15:3b-4). Paul said that more than 500 people had seen the risen Jesus, most of them still alive at the time of his writing.

We have not seen the risen Jesus ourselves, but we know what Easter is about—the resurrection of our Lord. Jesus died, was buried, and on the third day he came back to life. He was raised by the power of God. And that changes everything.

That is the point of Don Piper's account of *90 Minutes in Heaven*. Don says it is not his book that has the power to transform lives, but the message behind his book. It is the message of Easter: Jesus is alive. And everyone who believes in Jesus, even though they die, yet will live. Yes, Easter changes everything. This world is not all there is. This life is not all there is. We live for more than today. We live in the light of eternity. Death is not the final word. The grave could not hold Jesus, and the grave is not the end for those who believe. Don Piper said that he spent 90 minutes in heaven that January day of 1989, but God has promised us an eternity in heaven.

What does Easter mean to you? I pray it means that you have hope and peace and joy and love, because Jesus lives.

QUESTIONS FOR DISCUSSION/REFLECTION

1. Has Jesus ever appeared to you? If so, in what form and in what circumstances, and how did you know it was Jesus?
2. What was the significance of Jesus calling Mary by name?
3. Mary went and told the disciples, "I have seen the Lord." Have you ever told anyone about your experience with Jesus?
4. What is the meaning of Jesus ascending to the Father? What is the meaning of this event, not only for Jesus, but also for us?

CHAPTER 9

JESUS APPEARS TO THE DISCIPLES
(John 20:19-23)

It was still the first day of the week. That evening, while the disciples were behind closed doors because they were afraid of the Jewish authorities, Jesus came and stood among them. He said, "Peace be with you." After he said this, he showed them his hands and his side. When the disciples saw the Lord, they were filled with joy. Jesus said to them again, "Peace be with you. As the Father sent me, so I am sending you." Then he breathed on them and said, "Receive the Holy Spirit. If you forgive anyone's sins, they are forgiven; if you don't forgive them, they aren't forgiven." (John 20:19-21 CEB)

The disciples were behind closed doors. Mary Magdalene had told them that Jesus was alive, but they were still afraid. What if the Jewish authorities came after them? So, the doors of the house were locked, for fear of the Jews. But Jesus came and stood among them. (Never mind the locked doors!) Twice he said to them, "Peace be with you." How they needed peace after all they had experienced the past three days! His crucifixion was still a horrifying memory, and the news of his resurrection seemed too good to be true. But here was Jesus, in the disciples' midst, offering them peace.

They could hardly believe it. So, he showed them his hands and his side. Yes, it really was the Lord! They rejoiced; they were filled with joy. The signs of his suffering now were signs of his glory. He breathed on them. As God had breathed his breath to give life to the first human in Genesis 2, so now Jesus was giving new life in the gift of his Holy Spirit. And he was giving his followers work to do. As the Father had sent him, he was sending them, to offer forgiveness to all who would receive his grace.

FEAR AND DOUBT
(John 20:19-25)

It's called free-range parenting. The idea is to give children the freedom to learn, to grow, to discover the world, to make responsible decisions without their parents always hovering over them. It sounds like a worthy concept, but working out the details of free-range parenting is not easy.

I read about some free-range parents in Montgomery County, our neighbor in Maryland. They got into trouble with the authorities for allowing their children to walk home unaccompanied from a neighborhood park. This was the second time that the kids, ages 10 and 6, were stopped by the police while walking home by themselves. This second time the police took the children to Child Protective Services, where they were held for several hours. In the meantime, the parents were frantic because they did not know where their children were. The children were picked up because there is a law in Maryland that says any child under the age of 8 must be supervised by a responsible person who is at least 13 years old. The law applies to children in a building or a vehicle, but is unclear about whether it applies to children who are outside.

According to some studies, children are outside less than they used to be. Part of that is the allure of television, video games, and other indoor activities. But some of it may be due to overprotective parents who are afraid to let their children play outside without adult supervision. Any discussion of free-range parenting is likely to elicit strong opinions. I do not blame the police for wanting to protect the children, nor do I blame the parents for wanting to give their children freedom to play outside or walk in the neighborhood. The issue is finding the right balance between protection and freedom.

When I was a boy, I was outside a lot. I walked all over our neighborhood. During the school year I walked to school, about a mile from our house. When I got older, I rode my bike to school. A lot of kids did. Is the world a more dangerous place now than it was then? That is a good question.

According to FBI statistics, America actually has gotten safer in the last 30 years. Most major crime statistics are lower now than they were then. Crime is down, but our awareness of crime is way up. With 24-hour news on television and the Internet and our cell phones, when something bad happens, we hear all about it. When a child goes missing, it is all over the news, as it should be.

According to the National Center for Missing and Exploited Children, more than 421,000 children in America were reported missing in 2019. In most of those cases, the children were taken by a relative or an acquaintance, or they were teenagers who ran away from home. In most of those cases, the children were found. Of the 421,000 children reported missing, just over 100 were abducted by a stranger.

Any abduction is horrifying. We want our children to be safe. We want to protect them. But if parents are always hovering over their children, they will never learn to be independent; they will never really grow up. If we are so overprotective that we instill in our children a sense of fear, and a sense of doubt in their self-reliance, they will never mature and learn to take reasonable risks. Life is a risky business. Life is not always safe. Yes, there are dangers that we must remain aware of, but we were not meant to live in fear.

John 20 tells how that after the Resurrection, the disciples of Jesus were hiding behind closed doors in fear. They were afraid of the Jewish authorities. It was three days after Jesus had been crucified, and his followers were terrified they could be next. Mary Magdalene had told them that she had seen the Lord, but they doubted her testimony and were still scared. The doors of the house where they had gathered were shut, out of fear and doubt.

Now, of course, some fear is reasonable. The world is a dangerous place, and we should protect ourselves from unreasonable risks. But misplaced fear can stifle and ruin our lives. It can prevent us from living fully. Misplaced fear can keep us prisoners of our own paranoia, hiding behind emotional locked doors and never daring to venture out into the light of day.

In the midst of their fear and doubt, Jesus appeared to the frightened disciples and said, "Peace be with you." Into our world of fear, Jesus speaks a word of peace. It's not that life is suddenly safe. Jesus showed the disciples his hands and his side. He showed them the real wounds he had suffered when he was crucified. Jesus knew that life can be hard. It was hard for him. He suffered and died. But Jesus also knew about a peace that transcends the hard experiences of life. God is greater than the hardships, sufferings, fears, and doubts of life. Jesus was raised from the dead to calm our fears and our doubts and to give us peace.

Russell Kelso Carter was born in Baltimore in 1849. Although he had been raised in a Christian home, he struggled with doubts about making a personal decision for Christ. Finally, at the age of 15 he attended a prayer meeting at the military academy where he was a student. There, he committed his life to God. He went on to graduate from the academy (now Widener University) and became a teacher of chemistry and natural sciences. But even though he had committed his life to Christ and begun a teaching career, life was not easy.

At the relatively young age of 23, Kelso Carter began to have heart trouble. After several years of declining health, he moved to California and became a sheep rancher in an effort to strengthen his heart. By the age of 30, he was back at his parents' home in Baltimore in a near state of collapse. Desperate to try anything, he heard about a faith healer in Boston. He prayed that God would heal him, and then he traveled to see the preacher. Carter did experience healing and was able to resume his teaching career. He eventually became a Methodist minister and wrote a book, *Miracles of Healing*. But his health problems were not over.

Carter suffered a mental breakdown. The faith healer prayed over him, but Carter was not made well. Later he suffered an attack of malarial fever. Again, he prayed for healing. Although he recovered, Carter still felt chronically weak. He began to struggle with the whole idea of faith healing. He asked why some people were healed and others were not. He especially struggled with the knowledge that some people were not healed even when they believed in Christ and put their lives completely in God's hands. It wasn't that he had given up on believing in the healing power of prayer. He still believed that miracles of healing were possible, but he acknowledged that only a small percentage of people were completely healed in answer to prayer.

At the age of 49 Kelso Carter became ill again. This time he was diagnosed with "consumption" (or tuberculosis). Carter once again prayed for healing, but he also sought medical help. New medical advances had identified bacteria as the cause of the disease, and Carter received the latest medical treatments. Eventually he recovered from tuberculosis. That experience led Carter to realize that God works through medicine as surely as God works through prayer. Carter decided to seek medical training. He became a practicing physician in Baltimore around the turn of the 20th century. Kelso Carter continued to practice medicine in the Baltimore area until he died in 1928 at the age of 89 in Catonsville, Maryland.

Today we remember R. Kelso Carter not as a doctor, or even as a minister, but for a hymn he wrote, "Standing on the Promises." The hymn was written more than 130 years ago by a man who knew his share of fears and doubts. In fact, the second stanza begins, "Standing on the promises that cannot fail, when the howling storms of doubt and fear assail." Kelso Carter was able to overcome his own "howling storms" of doubt and fear through his faith in Jesus. Into Carter's troubled heart Jesus came and said, "Peace be with you." The teacher who became a preacher who became a physician experienced many times of doubt and fear in his life, but throughout he was able to stand upon the promises of God.

The risen Jesus came to the disciples in the midst of their own howling storms of doubt and fear. He spoke words of peace, and he showed them his hands and his side. They rejoiced when they saw the Lord. The risen Jesus still comes to us today and says, "Peace be with you." In the midst of our own doubt and fear, he calms the storm in our hearts and gives us peace. Life can be scary at times, but we are never alone. He comes to give us peace.

KNOWN BY THE SCARS
(John 20:19-23)

A Christian missionary was sent to Japan to tell the people about Jesus. Since he did not know the Japanese language yet, the missionary hired a translator to help him communicate with people. The only translator he could find was a Japanese man who taught English at the local high school. The interpreter was not a Christian himself, but he was willing to go with the missionary and translate the sermons as he preached. Things went well for a while; but then came the sermon on Easter Sunday. The missionary stood up and declared, "And on the third day Jesus arose from the dead." The translator hesitated, then turning to the missionary he said under his breath, "They are never going to believe this."

The Easter story has always been hard to believe. Even the disciples did not believe it at first. They had heard some strange reports. Mary Magdalene said she had seen Jesus in the garden outside the tomb where they had laid his body. Surely it was the delusion of an emotional, grief-stricken woman, the disciples must have thought. Then one of their own, the beloved disciple John, said he had seen the tomb empty. Grave robbers had struck, they must have thought.

The disciples simply could not believe that Jesus was alive. They had seen him die, if only from a distance. They knew about the nails driven into his hands and the spear thrust into his side. They knew he was dead and buried and gone. Now they feared they might be next. Maybe the Jewish authorities would not be satisfied with killing Jesus. Maybe they would go after his followers too.

So, the discouraged and frightened disciples had gathered in hiding behind locked doors. The terror they had felt when Jesus was first arrested was more intense now that Jesus had been crucified. On Sunday evening, three days after the Cross event, they had come together to huddle in fear and grief. Then, without warning, without expectation, without explanation, Jesus appeared.

The disciples did not recognize Jesus immediately. Maybe it was because they were not expecting to see him. Maybe Jesus had a different look about him, different from the way they had last seen him in agony on the cross. Whatever the reason, that was a common experience of people encountering the resurrected Christ. His followers did not recognize him immediately.

Mary Magdalene had seen him in the garden outside the empty tomb, but she assumed he was the gardener. It was only after Jesus spoke her name that she knew who he was. Two disciples walking along the road to Emmaus did not recognize Jesus when he came alongside them. They assumed he was just another traveler. It was only after he sat down to have dinner with them and said the blessing over the bread that they knew who he was. And here on Sunday night, the 10 disciples did not recognize Jesus either. (Judas, of course, was not there, for he had betrayed Jesus, and he committed suicide out of anguish for what he had done.) For some reason, one of the remaining 11 disciples, Thomas, was not there with the others. So, there were 10 of them gathered behind closed doors, perhaps in the same upper room where they had shared the last supper with Jesus on the night before he died.

When Jesus suddenly appeared in their midst, the disciples did not know what to think. It was only when Jesus showed them his scars, the nail prints in his hands and the spear wound in his side, that they knew who he was. All it took was the scars. In the end, Jesus was known by his scars.

Today we take the Cross for granted. We know how Jesus died, and it really does not shock us the way that it shocked his disciples. For them, his death was a scandal, a disgrace. Crucifixion was about the worst form of death imaginable. It was punishment reserved for the vilest criminals. For Jesus to die that way was worse than an embarrassment; it was a humiliating defeat. Not only that, but such a manner of death flew in the face of everything the disciples believed about God. They thought God was supposed to reward good people and punish bad people. They thought God was supposed to protect those who were faithful to him. It did not make sense for Jesus to suffer and die as he did. Jesus was the best person, the most faith-filled person they had ever known. How could something so bad happen to someone so good?

We still have a hard time understanding that today. Like those ancient Jews, we also believe that God is supposed to bless good people and punish bad people. We believe that God is supposed to reward those who are faithful to him and protect those who are trying to do the right thing. So, we don't understand why bad things happen to good people. We don't understand why people who are trying to live good, Christian lives sometimes experience undeserved pain and suffering. What we really don't understand is the nature of faith.

I remember hearing about a series of tornadoes that descended on parts of the South. One tornado slammed into a Methodist church in northeast Alabama that was packed with Palm Sunday worshippers. Tragically, 20 people were killed, and many more were injured. They died, not while they were doing something bad, but while they were doing something good, while they were worshipping God. The pastor of that church lost her 4-year-old daughter. Can you imagine a pastor losing 20 members of her congregation, and one of them being her own child? A television reporter asked the pastor if the tornado had destroyed her faith. The pastor replied quite the contrary: it was her faith that had kept her from being destroyed by those unimaginable losses.

Jesus showed his disciples the wounds in his hands and side because he wanted to be known by his scars. He wanted his followers to understand that faith in God does not protect us from all misfortune. Indeed, sometimes faith causes trouble in our lives because faith causes us to live God's way and not simply to follow the easy way of the crowd.

In his book, *The Death of the Messiah*, Raymond Brown says that Jesus was a "disturber of the religious structures of his day." Brown suggests that if Jesus were to appear in our time, he probably would be arrested and tried again. "Most of those finding him guilty would identify themselves as Christians," Brown writes, "and think they were rejecting an impostor." A suffering Messiah is still a scandal because we measure success in human terms. By human standards, an ignominious death on a cross was utter failure, not success at all. And so, we wonder, if faith in God does not keep bad things from happening to us, then what good is it? Faith did not keep bad things from happening to Jesus. If God did not spare his own Son, how dare we expect God to drop an invisible shield around us and protect us from all ill.

Could it be that faith in God has to do not so much with what happens to us, but with how we react to what happens to us? Could it be that faith gives us the power not to escape the problems of life, but to engage the problems of life in such a way that we are made better?

To be sure, God does not want any of us to suffer; God does not intentionally send tragedy into our lives. But we live in an imperfect world where tornadoes sometimes touch down on church buildings and innocent children perish beneath collapsed roofs. That is not what God wants. God wants the best for us. God wants us to work to create a world where tragedies such as that in Alabama do not happen. Maybe out of all this, meteorologists will develop early warning systems so that people can take cover before disaster strikes. Maybe builders will construct safer buildings, and people will be better educated about protecting themselves from severe weather.

But even when we do everything right, sometimes things go wrong. It's not that God is out to get us, or that God is falling down on the job in looking after us. It's just that we live in a world where nature is free and where people are free, and sometimes that freedom causes people to get hurt.

The resurrection of Jesus does not change the perils of life in this world. Even after Jesus was resurrected from the dead, he still bore the marks of suffering and death; he still bore the scars. That should be a comfort to us, knowing that God understands suffering and pain because Jesus endured more than most of us ever will. God understands what it is like to lose a child because he lost his only Son on a cross. The resurrection of Jesus does not remove all the perils of life, but it gives us the power to become stronger people. The scars are not a sign of God's abandonment, but the opposite: the scars are a sign of God's love.

In her novel, *The Thorn Birds*, Colleen McCullough tells the legend of a bird that sings just once in its life. The thorn bird sings only one time, but when it does, it sings more sweetly than any other creature on the face of the earth. McCullough writes:

> From the moment it leaves the nest it searches for a thorn tree, and does not rest until it has found one. Then, singing among the savage branches, it impales itself upon the longest, sharpest spine. And dying, it rises above its own agony to outsing the lark and the nightingale. One superlative song, existence the price. But the whole world stills to listen, and God in his heaven smiles. For the best is only bought at the cost of great pain…or so says the legend.

The story of the thorn bird is a beautiful legend, but the story of Jesus is absolute truth. His life was the sweetest song ever sung on his earth. And when he died the whole world stopped to listen. If that were the end of the story, his death would be nothing more than a tragedy. But that was not the end. On the third day, Jesus rose from the dead. And when he was raised to life by the power of God, the scars remained as eloquent testimony to the depth of his love.

No wonder the disciples were filled with joy when they saw the risen Jesus: they saw not just his face, but especially his scars. The nail prints in his hands, the wound in his side, were there for them—and they are there for us. Our Savior is risen, and he is known by his scars.

RECEIVE THE HOLY SPIRIT
(John 14:15-17, 16:5-15, 20:19-23)

There are three major days in the Christian year. The first two are easy to identify: Christmas and Easter. But what is the third most important day as far as the church is concerned? Mother's Day? Father's Day? Thanksgiving? The Fourth of July? Memorial Day? Labor Day? How about Groundhog Day? No, the third most important day of the Christian year is Pentecost.

My guess is that many Christians would never think about Pentecost as an important day because it is only a religious observance, without a corresponding secular tradition. At Christmas we have many popular traditions such as decorations, presents, Christmas trees, and Santa Claus; and at Easter we have flowers and Easter eggs and the Easter bunny. But Pentecost has no corresponding secular trappings.

Why is Pentecost so important? It's the day when we commemorate the gift of the Holy Spirit and the birth of the church. The Holy Spirit, sometimes called the Spirit of God or the Spirit of the Lord or simply the Spirit, is God's presence in the world. Because God is present in the world at all places and in all times, you may question why we need to talk about the Holy Spirit. It is true that God is everywhere. In Psalm 139:7-9 the Psalmist addressed God and asked: "Where can I go from your spirit? Or where can I flee from your presence? If I ascend to heaven, you are there; if I make my bed in Sheol, you are there. If I take the wings of the morning and settle at the farthest limits of the sea, even there your hand shall lead me, and your right hand shall hold me fast."

Of course, God is everywhere, because God is Spirit, not confined to the physical limits of the material world. Likewise, God's Holy Spirit is everywhere. God's Spirit was present at the dawn of creation, so the Holy Spirit of God has always been present. But from time to time, the Bible pictures God's Spirit being present in an especially focused or powerful way.

Certain key figures in the Old Testament were said to have received God's Spirit. The Spirit of the Lord came upon leaders such as Moses, Joshua, the judges, David, Elijah, and the prophets. Joel prophesied that God would pour out his Spirit on all flesh on the Day of the Lord.

In the New Testament, all four gospel writers describe the Spirit of God descending on Jesus at his baptism. Did this mean that God's Spirit was not with Jesus before his baptism? Of course not. Jesus was conceived by the Holy Spirit, and God's Spirit was with Jesus from the moment of his conception and throughout his life. But at his baptism, Jesus became aware of the presence of God's Spirit in a new, focused, powerful way. When Jesus was baptized in obedience to God's will for his life, it was as if the Spirit of God descended upon him like a dove. That is why a dove is sometimes a symbol of the Holy Spirit. There are other symbols of the Holy Spirit.

Sometimes the Holy Spirit is symbolized by wind or breath. That's because the word for spirit in Hebrew, *ruah*, and the word for spirit in Greek, *pneuma*, both have multiple meanings in each language. Both *ruah* and *pneuma* can be translated as spirit, or wind, or breath. Another symbol for the Spirit of God is fire.

When God encountered Moses in the wilderness, God's presence was represented by a fiery bush that was not consumed. After the exodus from Egypt, the Israelites were led by God's Spirit through the wilderness, and the visible signs of God's presence were a cloud by day and a pillar of fire by night. On the day of Pentecost in the New Testament, the Spirit of God descended on all the followers of Jesus like tongues of fire. So, fire was another symbol of God's Holy Spirit.

All these symbols—the dove, wind, breath, fire—picture something that cannot be described in literal terms. How do you describe Spirit? By definition, it is nonmaterial and thus cannot be seen or touched or felt in a physical way. But God is present through the Holy Spirit, and sometimes the Spirit of the Lord comes upon people in a more focused, powerful way.

When Jesus began his ministry, he said, "the Spirit of the Lord is upon me" (Luke 4:18). So, when Jesus was with his disciples, God's Spirit was present to them through Jesus. But Jesus knew that he would not be with them forever in a physical way to represent God's Spirit, so he prepared his disciples for his absence when they would experience God's presence through the Holy Spirit. On many occasions Jesus told his disciples that after he was gone, the Holy Spirit would come and take his place in their lives.

Jesus used yet another word for the Spirit of God, the Greek word *parakletos*, which means advocate / comforter / defender / instructor / guide. Jesus said that after he was gone, his disciples would not be abandoned. Rather, they would be comforted by an abiding spiritual presence that would never leave them.

Jesus Appears to the Disciples

The gospel writer John said that the risen Jesus breathed on the disciples and they received the Holy Spirit, similar to when God breathed life into a form of clay he had fashioned and the clay became a living person. Likewise, Jesus breathed the Holy Spirit into his disciples, and they became alive in a new and powerful way, more alive than they had ever been. Later, in the book of Acts, Luke described how the Holy Spirit came upon the disciples as the rush of a mighty wind.

They already had been made aware of God's presence when Jesus breathed into them the Holy Spirit after the Resurrection. But on the day of Pentecost the Spirit came upon them in such a forceful and dramatic way, they took on a boldness to witness for Christ that they had not had before. It was not that God's Spirit had been missing before. It was just that on Pentecost they became aware of God's Spirit as they had never been aware before.

In his video presentation, *The Search for Excellence*, Tom Peters talks about the railroad industry of the late 1800s in America. Toward the end of the 19th century, no business matched the financial and political dominance of the railroad companies. There was no competition for moving people or goods across this country other than the railroads. Then, around the turn of the 20th century, a new mode of transportation came along: the automobile. Incredibly, the railroad industry did not want to have anything to do with the fledgling automotive technology. Railroad companies were uniquely positioned to be at the forefront of developing this new means of transportation, but they refused to use their dominant position to become part of the automotive revolution. The problem, Peters argues, is that the railroad barons did not realize what business they were in. They thought they were in the train business when they really were in the transportation business. Because they did not understand their true purpose, the opportunity of a lifetime passed them by. The same thing happened with Swiss watchmakers around the middle of the 20th century.

At one time, the Swiss dominated the manufacture of watches and clocks worldwide. They controlled 90 percent of all revenues in the time-keeping industry. They made the most precise watch gears and clock springs in the world. Then something new came along called the Quartz movement. Guess who invented it—a Swiss watchmaker. But because this new type of timepiece had no gears or springs, the other Swiss watch and clock manufacturers wanted nothing to do with it. A Japanese company called Seiko, using this new technology, soon became the dominant watch manufacturer in the world. Today the Swiss account for less than 20 percent of time-keeping revenue. They missed a unique opportunity because they did not understand what business they were in. They thought they were in the business of manufacturing precise gears and springs, when they really were in the business of helping people tell time.

What business are we in as a church? Jesus has given us his Spirit to fulfill the mission left for his followers. And that mission is to continue the work he started. Every Christian, every believer who has given her or his life to Jesus Christ, has been given the gift of God's Spirit. But too often we are not aware of that Holy Spirit in our lives. Too often we are focused on other things. God wants to do a great work through us, and God has given us the power to do a great work, but it happens only as we allow God's Spirit to work through us. It happens when we focus on the purposes of God, rather than our own interests and desires. Jesus breathed on the disciples and said, "Receive the Holy Spirit." Jesus continues to breathe his Holy Spirit into the lives of all who believe in him. And just as Jesus gives new life to his followers, he gives us work to do: to proclaim the love of God and forgiveness for all who will receive his grace.

QUESTIONS FOR DISCUSSION/REFLECTION

1. The risen Jesus came and stood among his followers. In what ways does Jesus come and stand among us?
2. Two times the risen Jesus said to the disciples, "Peace be with you." How can we hear and receive his peace for our lives?
3. Why did Jesus show the disciples his hands and his side? What is the meaning for us?
4. In what ways is Jesus sending us into the world? What is our mission?
5. How does Jesus breathe his Holy Spirit into our lives?

CHAPTER 10

JESUS APPEARS TO THOMAS
(John 20:24-29)

> *A week later his disciples were again in the house, and Thomas was with them. Although the doors were shut, Jesus came and stood among them and said, "Peace be with you." Then he said to Thomas, "Put your finger here and see my hands. Reach out your hand and put it in my side. Do not doubt but believe." Thomas answered him, "My Lord and my God!" (John 20:26-28 NRSV)*

Thomas was not present that first Sunday night when Jesus appeared to his disciples. They told him they had seen the Lord, but Thomas would not believe them. He has been called "Doubting Thomas" ever since. But Thomas did not remain a doubter. The following Sunday night the disciples gathered again, and this time Thomas was there. The risen Jesus appeared among them again, and Thomas saw and believed. He simply wanted visible proof that Jesus was alive.

Thomas was no different from the rest of the disciples. But subsequent generations of believers, including us, believe that Jesus was raised based on the testimony of those who saw and believed. Jesus said we are blessed who have not seen but have come to believe.

BEYOND DOUBT
(John 20:24-29)

A "turn around" moment can change a life. It was a Wednesday morning in Memphis, Tennessee. Sean and Leigh Anne Tuohy were driving in the car with their son S.J. and their daughter Collins. They were about to pass Collins' school when Collins recognized "the new kid in school" who had just gotten off a city bus. The "kid" was hard to miss. He was 6 feet, 5 inches tall and weighed more than 350 pounds. Leigh Anne noticed that the teenager was inappropriately dressed for the weather. It was cold, with snow beginning to fall, but the young man was wearing just cut-off jeans and sneakers and a tee shirt. Plus, it didn't make any sense for him to be there because there was no school that day, the day before Thanksgiving.

Sean said he would have driven by at 35 mph and not given it a second thought, but Leigh Anne told him to turn around. That was all she said: "Turn around." They drove back to where the teenager was walking. Leigh Anne called out and invited him to get into the car. He was reluctant, but Leigh Anne insisted. Recognizing Collins in the back seat, the teenager got into the car. Leigh Anne asked him why he was there since school was closed that day. She asked him why he wasn't wearing proper clothes for such cold weather. He didn't really have an answer, something about heading to the school gym. She asked him to go home with her family so he could get something to eat and warm up, but the young man refused. He just asked them to drop him off at the Express Bus Stop.

The following Monday, Leigh Anne went to school to find out more about the new student. She had learned from Collins that his name was Michael, but that was about all she knew about him. The principal cautioned Leigh Anne not to get involved. He said it was not her business, and Michael probably wasn't going to make it in school anyway. Leigh Anne was undeterred. She went out and bought a new shirt and pants for Michael. The next day she sent Sean to the school to see if Michael was wearing the new clothes. Sean saw Michael sitting in the school lunchroom, but he wasn't eating. Sean figured that Michael didn't have money to buy lunch, so he bought a lunch card and had it given to Michael anonymously. The next day when Sean went to the school to check on Michael, he saw that "Big Mike" had enough food for about four lunches in front of him. The boy was obviously hungry.

Over the course of the next several months the Tuohys found out more about Michael. They learned that he did not have a home or a family. His mother was a crack addict, and his father wasn't around. They would later learn that his father had been murdered, shot, and thrown off an overpass. Michael had spent most of his childhood shuffled from one foster home to another. He went to 11 different schools in nine years. Michael often skipped school altogether. His freshman year of high school, he was absent 51 days. One of 12 children, Michael basically had been on his own most of his life. He had run away from the last foster home and was sleeping on the couch at the home of a friend's father. It was the friend's father who had gotten Michael admitted to this current school, a private Christian academy. Presumably, the school admitted Michael because they thought he would be an asset to the athletic program.

Eventually, Michael went to live with the Tuohys. Sean said, "It was his decision to stay at our house." Sean and Leigh Anne became his legal guardians. Unlike the foster homes he had been in, Michael became a part of the family. The Tuohys gave him his own room with his own bed. (Michael had never slept in a bed of his own.) Sean and Leigh Anne hired a private tutor to help Michael catch up on all the schoolwork he had missed. After a while, the Tuohys adopted Michael. He became a permanent member of their family. Leigh Anne said, "We did this one simple, random act of kindness. All we did was love him. We offered him hope, and we offered him love, and we offered him opportunity. And it changed his life." And it changed their lives too.

If this story sounds familiar, you may have seen the movie, *The Blind Side*, or read the book on which the movie was based. Michael is Michael Oher, a first-round draft pick of the Baltimore Ravens. After playing on the offensive line for the Ravens for five years, he played for the Tennessee Titans and then the Carolina Panthers. If Leigh Anne Tuohy had not told her husband to "turn around" that morning in Memphis in 2003,

Jesus Appears to Thomas

who knows what would have happened to Michael Oher? Who knows what would have happened to the Tuohys? A "turn around" moment can change a life.

In our scripture passage a "turn around" moment changed Thomas' life. Thomas, of course, was one of the 12 disciples of Jesus. But after Jesus was crucified, Thomas had just about given up hope. Maybe that's why he was not present when the risen Jesus first appeared to the other disciples.

It was Sunday evening, three days after Jesus had died. The disciples were afraid and discouraged, but Jesus appeared among them and said, "Peace be with you." Then Jesus showed them his hands and his side, which still bore the marks of his crucifixion. Seeing the wounds, they knew that it was not an apparition or a ghost. Jesus really was alive. Their doubt and fear were turned to joy. But Thomas was not there that Sunday night when Jesus appeared among them. So, when the disciples told Thomas, "We have seen the Lord," he did not believe them. He said, "Unless I see the mark of the nails in his hands and put my finger in the mark of the nails and my hand in his side, I will not believe."

I don't blame Thomas for not believing. I probably would not have believed it had I been there. I'm a doubter myself, or maybe I'm more of a skeptic. If something sounds too good to be true, I'm skeptical about it. I want proof, or at least I want convincing evidence. That's why I resonate with this story. I feel a kinship with Thomas. He just wanted some basis on which to believe.

A week later, the following Sunday night, the disciples had gathered again, and this time Thomas was with them. Once again the doors were shut, and once again Jesus came and stood among them. Once again Jesus said, "Peace be with you." Then he turned to Thomas. Jesus invited Thomas to put his finger in the marks of his hands and to place his hand on Jesus' side. Jesus said, "Do not doubt but believe." That was the "turn around" moment. Thomas stopped doubting and started believing. He exclaimed, "My Lord and my God!" It was a "turn around" moment that forever would change his life.

"Turn around" moments can change a life. There was no reason for Leigh Anne Tuohy to tell her husband Sean to "turn around" that cold day after they passed a big teenager walking along the road in Memphis. But looking back, Leigh Anne sees how God was speaking to her in that moment, telling her to get involved. Leigh Anne believes that God has been using their story to inspire others to turn around and help someone. Since they adopted Michael Oher, Leigh Anne and Sean Tuohy have gotten involved in the larger cause of children who need a forever family. Leigh Anne says there are more than 140,000 kids in America who don't have a permanent home. She and Sean are using the platform of their celebrity from the book and the movie to speak out for the cause of adoption. Now, they realize that not everyone can adopt a child, especially when that child is a teenager who stands 6 feet, 5 inches tall and and weighs 350 pounds. But everyone can do something to let a child know they care.

We don't know for sure what happened to Thomas after he met the risen Jesus face to face. We do know that he had his "turn around" moment. We know that he moved beyond doubt to faith. But what Thomas did after he confessed faith in Jesus is not recorded in the Bible. Early Christian traditions tell us, however, that Thomas became a missionary who carried the good news about Jesus to distant lands. Eusebius quotes the early church father Origen who said that Thomas carried the gospel to the Parthians, a people in the northern region of the country that we now know as Iran. A third-century book called *The Acts of Thomas* says that Thomas traveled to India in A.D. 52 and preached the gospel there. Indeed, many Christians in India today consider Thomas to be their patron saint.

Thomas was not the only disciple to experience a "turn around" moment. All the disciples moved beyond doubt to faith. Within a generation the early Christians carried the message of Jesus throughout the Roman Empire and beyond. Paul was by no means the only early Christian missionary. Someone, perhaps Peter, carried the gospel to Rome long before Paul ever got there. In fact, Paul himself had a "turn around" moment on the road to Damascus when he moved beyond doubt to faith in Jesus.

And so, the message of Jesus is about turning around. Today can be a "turn around" moment for you. Perhaps today you can move beyond doubt to faith. If you have never publicly professed your faith in Jesus and followed him as a believer in baptism, perhaps today is the moment you make that decision. Or maybe you have been a Christian for some time, but you are not a member of a church. Maybe this is the day you would join with a family of faith to serve Christ. Or maybe you are already a church member, but God is calling you to do something more to express your faith in him. Maybe this is the moment to "turn around" and get involved in whatever God is calling you to do. We may not see him with our eyes, but the spirit of the risen Christ is here, calling each of us to move beyond our doubt; to see with our hearts and believe. Jesus said that all who believe, even without seeing, will be blessed.

THOMAS: FROM DOUBT TO FAITH
(John 20:19-29)

There is a famous scene in Act III of Shakespeare's play, *Julius Caesar*, when Marc Antony delivers a funeral oration for the assassinated emperor:

> Friends, Romans, countrymen, lend me your ears;
> I come to bury Caesar, not to praise him.
> The evil that men do lives after them;
> The good is oft interred with their bones;
> So let it be with Caesar.

With this beginning, Marc Antony gives the impression he agrees that Caesar was an evil man who deserved to have been killed. In the rest of his speech, however, Marc Antony reminds the crowd of Caesar's good qualities and rouses them against the conspirators. Shakespeare was right: people are more likely remembered for mistakes they have made and wrongs they have done than for anything good they have accomplished. "The evil that men do lives after them; the good is oft interred with their bones."

Jesus Appears to Thomas

Consider, for example, our United States presidents over the past 60 years or so. In most cases we tend to remember their mistakes and failures more than their achievements and successes.

- John F. Kennedy is remembered for his personal charisma and the assassination that took his life. But he is also remembered for the Bay of Pigs fiasco that poisoned U.S. relations with Cuba, and for getting our country involved in the Vietnam War.
- Lyndon Johnson is remembered for his civil rights and Great Society legislation, but most of all he is remembered for escalating the war in Vietnam.
- Richard Nixon is remembered most of all for the Watergate scandal. The positive things he did, such as ending the Vietnam War and opening relations with China, are overshadowed by the scandal that forced him to resign from office.
- Gerald Ford sought to restore trust in government, but he is remembered for pardoning Nixon.
- Jimmy Carter advanced the cause of human rights around the world, but is remembered for high inflation and the Iran hostage crisis.
- Ronald Reagan helped hasten the collapse of communism in many countries, but his fiscal policies, which even his own vice president once labeled "voodoo economics," may have sown the seeds for subsequent economic crises. "Trickle-down economics" only widened the income disparities between the rich and the poor, and the deregulation of the financial industry led our country to the brink of another crisis.
- George H.W. Bush was wildly popular after the first Gulf War, but his economic policies led to his defeat after only one term.
- Bill Clinton is remembered more for his affair with a White House intern than for his budget surpluses and a robust economy.
- George W. Bush rallied our country after 9/11, but he probably will be remembered more for starting a war with Iraq under premises that proved not to be true. There were no weapons of mass destruction.
- (If I were to talk about Barack Obama, Donald Trump, and Joe Biden, you might think I am getting too political. So I'll stop here, but you get the idea.)

The point is that people are often remembered more for what they did wrong than for what they did right. A case in point is our scripture passage and the apostle Thomas, who forever will be known as the doubter. When Jesus appeared to his disciples on the night after the Resurrection, for some reason Thomas was not present. When the disciples told him that they had seen Jesus alive, Thomas did not believe them.

Who could blame Thomas for being a doubter? All the disciples doubted the Resurrection at first. When the women came back from the tomb on Sunday morning and told the disciples that Jesus had been raised from the dead, the disciples dismissed the women's report as nothing more than an idle tale. So, Thomas only wanted what the other disciples had already received: visible proof that Jesus really was alive. Yet, Thomas will forever be known as "Doubting Thomas." The negative is often remembered more than the positive. That one moment of doubt has come to define the life of Thomas in the minds of many people.

Yes, Thomas doubted at first, but Jesus was not dismayed by Thomas' disbelief. That was why Jesus appeared a second time to the disciples, a week later, when Thomas was there. This repeat appearance seems to have been for Thomas' benefit. Jesus gave Thomas the same opportunity to believe that had been given the other disciples. Sure enough, after Jesus appeared and invited Thomas to put his finger in the nail prints and touch the wound in Jesus' side, Thomas believed. He proclaimed, "My Lord and my God!" Upon meeting the risen Christ, Thomas moved from doubt to faith.

So, I think it is a little simplistic, and frankly unfair, to label Thomas a doubter. He was skeptical, but who wouldn't be? Rather, we gain insight into Thomas' character not from this story alone, but also from two other stories about Thomas in the Gospel of John.

First, in John 11 we read that Lazarus, a good friend of Jesus, was ill. His sisters Mary and Martha sent a message to Jesus, "Lord, he whom you love is ill." Rather than rushing to Lazarus' side, however, Jesus delayed and went to Bethany.

After two days Jesus said to his disciples, "Let us go to Judea again." The disciples were alarmed. They did not want Jesus to go anywhere near Judea. Just days before, some Jews in the region had taken up stones to kill Jesus. The disciples knew that going back to Judea, even to attend to a sick friend, would be extremely dangerous. After Jesus told them that Lazarus was already dead, it made no sense to them to go back to Bethany. Why risk it if Lazarus already had died? But Jesus said he was going. Thomas said to his fellow disciples, "Let us also go, that we may die with him." Thomas did not sound like much of a doubter then, did he?

Thomas played a role in another story in the Gospel of John. In chapter 14, Jesus shared a last supper with his disciples on the night before he died. During the meal Jesus spoke about his coming death, telling them:

> "Do not let your hearts be troubled. Believe in God, believe also in me. In my Father's house are many dwelling places. If it were not so, would I have told you that I go to prepare a place for you? And if I go and prepare a place for you, I will come again and will take you to myself, so that where I am, you may be also. And you know the way to the place where I am going." (vv. 1-4)

Thomas said to Jesus, "Lord, we do not know where you are going. How can we know the way?" It was not that Thomas doubted Jesus; he simply did not understand. Jesus replied, "I am the way, and the truth, and the life. No one comes to the Father except through me. If you know me, you will know my Father also. From now on you do know him and have seen him" (John 14:6-7). It was Thomas' honest question that prompted Jesus to declare clearly who he was: "I am the way, and the truth, and the life."

From these stories the picture that emerges of Thomas is not so much that of a doubter as that of a realist. When Jesus declared his intention to return to Judea, Thomas realized what that meant. He knew that those who had tried to kill Jesus would try again to kill him. That was why Thomas said, "Let us also go, that we may die with him." In the upper room, when Jesus talked about going to his Father's house, Thomas did not understand what Jesus meant. How could Jesus go to his Father's house? Like the other disciples, the Cross was incomprehensible to Thomas. So, ever the realist, Thomas asked, "Lord, how can we know the way if we do not know where you are going?" It was not the question of a doubter, but the question of a realist who did not yet understand that Jesus' coming death on the cross would provide the way to the Father.

What emerges from these stories about Thomas is a man of great courage whose feet were planted firmly in reality. That was why he doubted Jesus was alive. Thomas knew that Jesus really had died on the cross. But when given the same opportunity to see the risen Christ for himself that the other disciples had been given, Thomas moved from doubt to faith. We should remember Thomas more for his faith than for his doubt.

I can identify with Thomas because I tend to be more of a realist than an idealist. I am skeptical about things that are hard to believe. I think there is value in honest doubt because it keeps us grounded in reality. But Thomas was also a man of faith. He realized that doubt can only take you so far. There comes a time when you have to trust in something, or Someone. And that was what Thomas did. He placed his faith in Jesus. Doubting Thomas became believing Thomas.

The New Testament does not tell us what happened to Thomas after that, but early church traditions say that he became a great missionary, taking the gospel east as far as India. Traditions also say that Thomas was killed as a martyr in India, in the city known today as Madras, where later a basilica was dedicated in his name.

Doubts need not be the end of faith. Sometimes doubts can lead to faith. Seeing the risen Jesus, Thomas moved from doubt to faith. But Jesus said, "Blessed are those who have not seen and yet have come to believe." Jesus was talking about us. We are blessed when we believe. Like Thomas, may we be remembered as people of faith too.

DOUBT AND FAITH
(John 20:24-31)

Every so often I meet someone who has drifted away from the church. For example, I was talking with a lady who had grown up in the Roman Catholic Church. In her early years she went to Mass every Sunday, she went to Confession regularly, she attended Catechism classes as a child, she took first Communion—she went through the steps that were expected of her to be a Catholic. But as she grew older, she stopped attending Mass and doing the other things, and she drifted away from the church. Part of it was that she had begun to think for herself, and she found that she could not accept all the teachings of the Catholic Church. Part of it was the natural pulling away from organized religion that many young people go through as they begin to grow up and assert their independence. For whatever reason, this woman was no longer affiliated with the Catholic Church—or any church. She told me she wanted to believe in something, but her doubts had gotten in the way.

Our scripture passage is about the most famous doubter in the Bible. His name was Thomas, and he was one of the original 12 disciples of Jesus. In reality, Thomas was not any less reliable than the other disciples. They all had their failings. They all ran out on Jesus when he was arrested in the Garden of Gethsemane the night before he died. They scattered like sheep without a shepherd. Peter did follow at a distance to the place where Jesus was being questioned after his arrest but, there in the courtyard of the high priest, Peter denied three times that he even knew Jesus. John, the Beloved Disciple, was present at the foot of the cross when Jesus died, but like the others he then went into hiding.

On the Sunday after the Crucifixion most of the disciples had come together to share their mutual grief and to console one another. When the women returned from the tomb with the news that Jesus had been raised from the dead, the disciples did not believe them. But later that evening, as most of the disciples were gathered behind closed doors for fear of the Jews, the risen Jesus came and stood among them. Most of the disciples were there, but not all of them. Judas was not there because he had killed himself out of remorse for betraying Jesus. Also, for some reason, Thomas was not there.

Later, when the disciples told Thomas that the risen Jesus had appeared to them, he did not believe it. Thomas was skeptical, just as all of the disciples had been skeptical when the women first told them about the empty tomb. Thomas was a doubter, but all of them were doubters at first.

Doubt is not always a bad thing. Sometimes it's a good thing. Doubt keeps us from getting sucked in by some get-rich-quick scheme that seems too good to be true. Doubt keeps us from believing in some screwball religious leader who wants us to follow him rather than following Jesus. Doubt keeps us grounded in reality rather than being carried away by emotions or wishful thinking. Sometimes doubt is a good thing. The problem is when doubt keeps us from seeing the truth.

Every year the results of the American Religious Identification Survey are released. This is a nationwide survey that asks Americans about their religious beliefs. One of the questions included in the survey is: "What is your religion, if any?" According to the latest survey, although the American population still identifies itself as predominantly Christian, Americans are less Christian than they used to be. For example:

- In 1990, 56 percent identified themselves as Protestant. In 2019, only 35 percent identified themselves as Protestant.
- In 1990, 25 percent identified themselves as Roman Catholic. In 2019, that number had dropped to 22 percent. Generic Christian churches, including Pentecostal and Charismatic, make up another 10 percent.
- In 1990, 9 percent claimed no religious affiliation at all. In 2019, the number of "nones" had increased to 21 percent.

An increasing number of Americans claim no religion at all. One indication of this lack of attachment to any religion is the number of those surveyed who said they do not expect their families to conduct a religious funeral for them at their deaths. More than a quarter of Americans do not expect a religious funeral—no reference to God or heaven or any hope beyond this earth.

For some reason, or maybe for many reasons, more and more people are opting out of organized religion. Maybe church does not seem relevant to their lives. Or maybe they are just too busy or interested in other things to think about religion. Maybe some people had negative religious experiences in the past and have now given up on religion.

I read an interview with the then-head of the Unitarian Universalist Association, William Sinkford. The Unitarian Universalist religion is the faith tradition where he could call himself an atheist and still serve as an ordained minister. Sinkford said that he used to see himself as an atheist, but then he felt a spiritual presence during a family tragedy. So, after the experience, he stopped calling himself an atheist, but Unitarian Universalists are not required to believe in God. Belief in a higher power is not one of their seven defining principles. They believe in a faith of deeds, not creeds. You might say that Unitarian Universalists are kind of a way station between the church and no religion at all. Sinkford said that many adult Unitarian Universalists came to that faith after negative experiences in other religious traditions, primarily Christian churches: they could bring all their questions and doubts with them.[1] At their best, Unitarian Universalist congregations try to be hospitable and inclusive of everyone. Questions and doubts are welcomed in a faith tradition with the motto, "deeds, not creeds."

Many people have been alienated by negative church experiences. They have felt hurt and wounded by judgmental attitudes. They have been turned off by dogmatic belief systems they cannot accept. They have felt condemned for having honest doubts. Maybe that is why the number of people with no religious preference is rising.

Jesus came not to condemn but to save. Jesus did not condemn Thomas for his doubts. Instead, Jesus appeared to the disciples again the following Sunday, and this time Thomas was with them. This repeat resurrection appearance was for Thomas' benefit. Jesus wanted to give Thomas the opportunity to overcome his doubts, so that he could see for himself and believe. But then, thinking about people like us, Jesus said, "Blessed are those who have not seen and yet have come to believe."

That is where we are. We have not seen the risen Christ in a visible way, because even if Jesus were to appear among us, how would we recognize him? We do not know what he looked like when he walked this earth. Yet, through eyes of faith, we do recognize his presence. Jesus is present wherever two or three are gathered in his name. Jesus in present in the least of these, wherever hurting people are helped. Jesus is present in the bread and cup of the Lord's Supper. Jesus is present as we open the scriptures and read God's word. Jesus is present in many ways, but we see with eyes of faith in order to believe.

I saw a cartoon once of two men going door to door handing out tracts. They were standing in front of a door and the lady inside said with a puzzled look on her face, "This pamphlet is blank." One of the men replied, "We're atheists." If there is no God, then the pamphlet is blank; there is nothing to write; there is no good news to share. Doubt alone is not enough to live on. We need something, we need Someone, to believe in. And the good news is that Someone has come to us, not to resolve all our doubts, but to offer us himself. And all who come to believe in him have life in his name.

QUESTIONS FOR DISCUSSION/REFLECTION

1. Why do you think Thomas was unwilling to believe the other disciples when they told him, "We have seen the Lord"?
2. In what sense is seeing believing?
3. How can we believe if we have not seen?
4. Jesus told Thomas, "Do not doubt but believe." Can we believe and still have doubts?
5. Jesus said, "Blessed are those who have not seen and yet have come to believe." Who do you think Jesus was talking about?

NOTE

[1] *dcexaminer*, March 29, 2009.

CHAPTER 11

THE LAST BREAKFAST
(John 21:1-14)

> *Early in the morning, Jesus stood on the shore, but the disciples did not realize it was Jesus. He called out to them, "Friends, haven't you any fish?" "No," they answered. He said, "Throw your net on the right side of the boat and you will find some." Jesus said to them, "Come and have breakfast." None of the disciples dared ask him, "Who are you?" They knew it was the Lord. (John 21:4-6a, 12 NIV)*

Fish for breakfast! This story of Jesus' post-resurrection appearance in Galilee is part of the epilogue to John's Gospel. The Fourth Gospel appears to end with the last two verses of chapter 20: "Now Jesus did many other signs in the presence of his disciples, which are not written in this book. But these are written so that you may come to believe that Jesus is the Messiah, the Son of God, and that believing you may have life in his name" (vv. 30-31). But chapter 21 adds another story, with another ending in verses 24-25. So, as John begins with a prologue in chapter 1, John ends with an epilogue in chapter 21.

In John 21:14 we read: This was now the third time that Jesus appeared to the disciples after he was raised from the dead. The first time was recorded in John 20:19-23, when Jesus appeared to the disciples in Jerusalem on the Sunday night after after he had been raised. The second appearance is in John 20:26-29, a week later when Thomas was with them. This third appearance of the risen Jesus to the disciples was in Galilee. As he had done on the night before he died, Jesus served as the host for a final meal, except this time it was breakfast rather than supper. Giving them bread and fish also was reminiscent of the feeding of the multitude in John 6:1-15, the only miracle recorded in all four gospels.

BREAKFAST WITH JESUS
(John 21:1-14)

On April 12, 2015, a 25-year-old African-American man named Freddie Gray was arrested by the Baltimore police. He was charged with possessing a knife. While he was being transported in a police van, Gray sustained spinal cord injuries from which he subsequently died. After Freddie Gray died, my wife Linda asked me if I was going to talk about Baltimore in my sermon on Sunday. I told her I would rather not. It seems that I had been preaching about racial justice repeatedly for several years. And basically, I was "preaching to the choir." Our congregation was not the problem. We did not just talk about reconciliation and Christian love in our church; we sought to live it. But what has been going on in the larger society around us is our concern.

Since Freddie Gray's death, a number of other African Americans have been killed by police: Philando Castile in 2016, Jordan Edwards in 2017, Botham Jean and Stephon Clark in 2018, Atatiana Jefferson in 2019, George Floyd and Breonna Taylor in 2020, and Daunte Wright in 2021.

Baltimore, Maryland is not Ferguson, Missouri or Minneapolis, Minnesota. It's not a black/white issue in Baltimore. When Freddie Gray died, most of the Baltimore leaders were African American, including the mayor and the president of the city council and the police commissioner. More than half of the Baltimore police force is African American. It is true that the percentage of white police officers in Baltimore is higher than the percentage of white citizens, but that is the demographic ratio in most cities. Justice demands that we seek to find out what happened when Freddie Gray was injured in police custody. If the injuries that led to his death were avoidable, then those who were responsible should be held accountable. But rioting, looting, arson, and attacks upon police officers have nothing to do with justice.

I thank God for police officers who put their lives on the line to maintain order in our communities. No doubt, in some places, police need to be more respectful toward citizens. Likewise, in some places, citizens need to be more respectful of police. But as we saw in Baltimore, without justice and order, there is chaos. When chaos happens, schools in Baltimore close and businesses are shut down and the Orioles cancel baseball games or play in an empty stadium or move games to other cities. When chaos happens, people stay away from Baltimore, and people who live in Baltimore are afraid to go about their normal lives. Chaos is not what God intended when he made us. God brought order out of chaos when he created the world, and God wants us to live together in harmony and peace. God's intention for us is not chaos, but community.

The epilogue to John's Gospel tells a story about community and fellowship shared between some of the disciples and Jesus. Seven of the disciples were out on the Sea of Galilee (also known as Tiberias). It was just after daybreak, following a long night of fishless fishing. The risen Jesus appeared to them along the shoreline, but they did not know it was Jesus. He called out to them and said, "You have no fish, do you boys?" "No," they replied. Jesus said, "Cast your net on the other side of the boat, and you will find some." They did what he said, and the net was filled with so many fish they could hardly haul it in.

"Who is that guy?" the disciples asked one another. John said to Peter, "It is the Lord!" Then Peter put his garment back on, jumped out of the boat into the water, and swam ashore. The other disciples rowed the boat to the beach, dragging the net full of fish with them. Jesus was waiting for them on the shore, standing over a charcoal fire. There was fish grilling on the fire, along with bread. Jesus invited them to add some of the fish they had caught to the meal he was preparing. The net was full of fish, yet the net was not torn. Jesus said, "Come and have breakfast." He took the bread and gave it to them. He did the same with the fish.

The Last Breakfast

This breakfast with Jesus was more than a meal; it was almost like communion. It was a celebration of community between the risen Jesus and his astonished disciples. Breakfast with Jesus: What could be better than that?

This is a wonderful story, but what does it mean—especially in the context of our troubled world today? The story reminds us that Jesus came to create community, to overcome barriers that divide us from one another, to create ties that bind us to one another.

The net full of fish is symbolic. According to John, there were 153 large fish, and even though there were so many, the net was not torn. What was it about the number 153? Did someone count all the fish, or was the number symbolic? Some scholars contend that in the ancient world it was believed there were 153 kinds of fish. Now we know the number of kinds of fish is much larger than that, but the 153 had symbolic meaning. If every kind of fish was in the net, and yet the net was not torn, that says something powerful about community: There is room in the community for everyone. Jesus created an inclusive community where no one would be excluded. That's what the church is—a community of love centered around Jesus that excludes no one.

Frankly, if it were up to me, there would be people that I would like to exclude. I'd exclude those rioters in Baltimore who set fires and looted stores and hurled rocks at police officers. But Jesus is willing to forgive every sinner who comes to him in faith. If it were up to me, I'd exclude police officers who violate the trust placed in them by abusing their authority. But Jesus is willing to forgive every sinner who comes to him in faith. The net is filled, but the net is not torn. There is room at the Cross for everyone.

Jesus appeared on the shore at daybreak after his disciples had spent all night on the sea and caught nothing. The disciples were tired and hungry and frustrated, but Jesus had breakfast waiting for them when they reached the shore. You see, Jesus really cared about them. He really cared about their work. Most of them were professional fishermen. That's what they did for a living. Jesus did not disparage their work. He didn't call to them on the sea and say, "Come on in, I've got more important work for you to do." This wasn't recreational fishing; this was their livelihood. Jesus affirmed their work, and he helped them to do it better. He told them to throw their net on the other side of the boat. He supported them in their labors. What they could not do on their own, they could do with help from Jesus.

Jesus not only cared about their work, but he also cared about their well-being. They had been fishing all night but had caught nothing. They were tired, frustrated, and hungry. Jesus fixed breakfast for them! But it wasn't a handout. Jesus respected their dignity. He invited them to add some of the fish they had caught to the meal. He offered them a partnership. Jesus cared about both their physical and emotional well-being. He cared about the totality of their lives.

Not only did Jesus care about the disciples' work and their well-being, but he also cared about their relationship with him. The meal almost had communion overtones. He took the bread and gave it to them. He did the same with the fish. It was reminiscent of Jesus feeding the five thousand with the loaves and fish. The purpose of that breakfast, or of any communion meal, is to gather people around Jesus. Every time we share the

Lord's Supper it's not exactly "Breakfast with Jesus," but it's communion with Jesus. It's an expression of our communion with God and our community with each other in the family of faith.

Jesus really cared about his disciples, and Jesus really cares about us. He cares about what we do. He cares about our work, our family life, the activities and pursuits that give our lives meaning and purpose. Jesus cares about our well-being. He cares if we are hungry or in need, tired or frustrated, sick or troubled. The totality of our lives really matters to Jesus. Most of all, Jesus cares about our relationship with him, and our relationships with each other. That's why he said, "As often you eat the bread and drink the cup, do this in remembrance of me." When we gather around the Lord's Table, we remember what Jesus did for us, and we express our community with one another as brothers and sisters in Christ.

I was troubled and saddened by what went on in Baltimore in 2015. I was troubled and saddened by the death of Freddie Gray and by the rioting that followed. Such protests and unrest are signs of a tragic lack of community. They are evidence of tremendous mistrust and broken relationships between the police department and many of the citizens of Baltimore. And that lack of community, trust, and relationships has resulted in chaos. But there is a way out of chaos.

Yes, we still seek justice for Freddie Gray. Of the six officers involved in his arrest and transport and injuries, none was convicted of a crime. The city of Baltimore did reach a financial settlement with Freddie Gray's family, but the larger issue is building community. The larger challenge is restoring trust and nurturing relationships. It's not just for the folks in Baltimore, but what all of us are called to do as followers of Jesus Christ. It's a call to peace with God, and peace with one another. Like spokes in a wheel, the closer we come to Jesus the closer we come to each other.

FISH FOR BREAKFAST?
(John 21:1-14)

My Uncle Jim had a house in Cayucos, California, overlooking Morrow Bay, right on the Pacific Ocean. When our son Marc was 8 years old, and our daughter Amy was an exchange student in France, Linda and Marc and I and my parents visited my uncle and aunt. Marc was interested in fishing at the time, so my father and my uncle took him out on a little boat to do some angling in the ocean. After several hours, they came back with quite a catch. I don't remember what kind of fish they caught, but we had fresh fish for dinner that night. The next morning, we woke up to the smell of fish cooking on the stove for breakfast. Now, I like fish—fried, broiled, grilled, and baked—but I don't particularly like the smell of fish the first thing in the morning. Marc was a little more blunt in his reaction. He said, "Fish for breakfast? Yuk!" Fortunately, Uncle Jim did not take offense. He knew that not everyone likes fish for breakfast. But some people do; some people like it a lot.

When Linda and I were in Hawaii, we noticed that some of the hotels offered a traditional Japanese breakfast. We did not know what a traditional Japanese breakfast was, but now we do. It includes steamed rice, green tea, and something called miso soup, made out of soybeans. It can also feature pickles, spinach, and raw eggs. It also includes fish. In a couple of the hotels, it was grilled salmon, but I suppose it could be other kinds of fish. So, for many Japanese, fish for breakfast is a welcome item on the menu.

Apparently, the disciples of Jesus enjoyed fish for breakfast. That is not surprising since many of them were fishermen. In that part of Palestine, the best time for fishing was at night, so it was not unusual for fishermen to come in with their boats and nets early in the morning after fishing all night. Presumably, it would not be unusual to prepare some of their catch for breakfast. The problem in our scripture passage was that the disciples did not have any catch after fishing all night. They had thrown their nets into the sea time and again, but their nets had come up empty.

In the half-light of the early dawn a stranger appeared on the shore and called out to them. In reality, he was not a stranger at all; he was the risen Jesus, but they did not recognize him at first. Perhaps being a hundred yards from the shore they were too far out to see the features of his face. Or maybe they were looking into the rising sun and all they could see was the silhouette of a figure on the beach. In any case, it was the resurrected Jesus, but they did not know it was Jesus.

Jesus called out to the disciples from the water's edge. "Young men," he said, "you haven't caught any fish, have you?" "No," they shouted back. "Cast your net on the other side of the boat," Jesus replied. They did what he said, and suddenly there were so many fish in their net that they could hardly haul it into the boat. The disciple whom Jesus loved, presumably John, said to Peter, "It is the Lord!" Peter, who had stripped off his outer garment while fishing, put his tunic back on and dove into the water to swim ashore. Perhaps he thought it would have been disrespectful to greet Jesus without proper clothes on.

The others rowed the boat to the shore. Jesus had a charcoal fire going, with some fish already grilling on it, along with some bread. Jesus invited the disciples to bring some of the fish they had caught and add them to what was already cooking. Simon Peter hauled the net ashore, and it was bulging with 153 fish. Amazingly, the net was not torn. When the fish were ready, Jesus said, "Come and have breakfast." It was like a communion meal. Jesus took bread and gave it to them, and he did the same with the fish. Instead of bread and wine, it was bread and fish. Breakfast with Jesus: it was a meal they would never forget.

This is a wonderful story, but what does it mean? The story has obvious communion overtones, as did the earlier story of the feeding of the five thousand beside the Sea of Galilee. In both stories, Jesus took bread and gave it to those present. The story of the feeding of the five thousand also featured a miraculous meal of fish. Any time people share a meal with Jesus, it's communion. But beyond the communion references, what does the story mean?

Let's look again at the miraculous catch of fish. The disciples had fished all night but caught nothing. Suddenly, at Jesus' command, they cast their net on the other side and their net was full. Fishing is a metaphor for the work that Jesus called his disciples to do. At one point, Jesus had told them they would become fishers of men. Fishing all night without catching any fish represented trying to do the work that Jesus had called them to do in their own power and in their own way.

Whether it is living the Christian life, or doing the work of the church, or raising a family, or being a witness for Christ in the workplace, or anything else, if we try to do it in our own power, our efforts will not succeed. But when we work according to the calling of Christ and live according to his will, our efforts will be rewarded. So, this story is about how we live the Christian life. If we try to live in our own strength and using only our own wits, it will be like fishing all night and catching nothing. But if we listen for Jesus' voice and follow his directions for our lives, our nets will be filled to overflowing.

So, this story is not only about fishing, but also about living the Christian life. We are called to live in partnership with Jesus. Did you notice that Jesus already had fish cooking on the charcoal fire when the disciples came ashore? Jesus already had started breakfast, but he invited the disciples to bring the fish they had caught and add them to the fire. That is the partnership involved in Christian living. Jesus does his part, and we do our part. He calls us to bring what we have and add it to the enterprise. Jesus is there to help us and provide for our needs, but he invites us to contribute too. Jesus invites us to bring our natural talents, gifts, abilities, and interests and use them in his service. Jesus invites us to bring our fish and add them to the fire.

The Christian life is not a one-way street. It's not just a matter of attending church and receiving what Jesus has to give. Jesus invites us to contribute too. We all have some fish to add to the breakfast. We all have something to place upon the fire. The church is not "them" and what they can do for me. The church is "us" and what we can do for each other and for God.

Perhaps the most intriguing detail of this story is the number of fish the disciples caught in their net: 153. Scholars have long debated the meaning of the number 153. Some have concluded that it was simply the actual number of fish in the net. Maybe one of the disciples counted all the fish and the total came to 153. But why would John include that detail, unless the number 153 had some further meaning?

Augustine noted that the number 153 is the sum of the integers of the numbers from 1 to 17. I got out my calculator and added them up: $1 + 2 + 3 + 4 + 5\ldots$, all the way to 17, and sure enough they add up to 153. So, in some sense, the number 153 represents totality. There is another possible explanation.

Ancient Greek zoologists believed there were 153 different species of fish. Of course, we know now that there are many more different species of fish, but in the ancient world 153 represented all the varieties of fish in the sea. Thus, in another way, 153 was a number representing totality.

Notice that the net was bulging with 153 fish, but the net did not break. I think the net represents the church, and the 153 fish represents all the people in the church. The 153 represents all the different kinds of people in the church. Young and old, rich and poor, educated and less educated, women and men, people from every nation, every racial group, every ethnic background, every social status—that is what the church is supposed to be. The church is supposed to be represented by all the peoples of the world.

The church is like the bulging net with 153 different kinds of fish. The net is filled, and the net is not torn. There is room in the church for all of us.

THE LAST BREAKFAST
(John 21:1-14)

Hanging on the walls of our dining room are blue dishes. They are souvenir plates from various tourist attractions from around the country. Even though some of the dishes are quite old, I doubt they are worth a lot of money. But they are worth a lot to me. The blue plates originally belonged to my grandmother. Every time our family would take a vacation trip, we would search out the local gift shop and bring back a blue plate and give it to her. My grandmother used the blue plates. Every time we had a meal at her house, we ate off those plates.

My grandmother was especially known in our family for her breakfasts. Most of the time when someone had a birthday, we would celebrate over breakfast at her house. We had homemade biscuits, so tender and flaky they fell apart in your hands. There was a sweet concoction called sugar syrup, made primarily out of sugar and water, and also sausage, bacon, and eggs. And always, there were the blue plates.

It was something of an adventure to finish your meal and clean your plate so that you could get down to the picture and see what site you had been eating from. It could be the Governor's Palace in Williamsburg, Virginia or the Alamo in San Antonio, Texas or the Washington Memorial Chapel in Valley Forge, Pennsylvania or Old Fort Harrod in Harrodsburg, Kentucky or Faneuil Hall in historic Boston or the Grand Canyon in Arizona.

After my grandmother died in 1984, my mother asked me what I wanted from her house. All I wanted were the blue plates. My mother was afraid to ship them, so she brought them a few at a time, carrying them by hand on the airplane every time she came to Maryland to visit us. Most of the time, breakfast is an ordinary meal, but sometimes breakfast can have special meaning. Such is the case for me with my grandmother's blue plates. Such was the case for the disciples and a special breakfast they shared beside the Sea of Tiberias.

You recall that on the night of the Resurrection, Jesus appeared to his disciples in a room in Jerusalem. On that first occasion, Jesus appeared to 10 of them who were in hiding behind closed doors. Then a week later, Jesus appeared again to the same 10, plus Thomas. Then, sometime later, seven of the disciples were back in their old stomping ground. Most of them originally came from the region around the Sea of Galilee, or the Sea of Tiberias as it was sometimes called. Jerusalem was not their home, so eventually, even though they had met the risen Jesus in Jerusalem, they went back up north to their homes and their work, back to their families and their friends, back to everything that was routine and familiar.

If we read between the lines, we see that the resurrection of Jesus still had not sunk in for the disciples. They knew that Jesus was alive and were happy about that. But they were having a hard time getting used to the fact that Jesus was not around in a physical way. They still did not understand what the Resurrection meant for them. And so, they went back to the things they did understand. They went back to fishing. At least four of the disciples had made their living as fishermen, and the others, being from Galilee, probably knew something about angling too. If you grew up around the water, it would be hard not to know something about fishing. Not sure what to do next, Simon Peter said, "I'm going fishing." And the others went too. It was Simon Peter, Thomas called the Twin, Nathanael of Cana in Galilee, the sons of Zebedee, and two other disciples (John 21:2).

It was night when they set out in the boat, apparently because night was a good time for fishing. But even though some of them were professionals and they had been fishing most of their lives, they did not catch a thing. All night they cast their nets into the water, and all night they drew them back into the boat empty. Can you imagine their frustration?

I remember when our son Marc tried fishing with his friends Jeremy and Gary Miles at the Miles boys' grandparents place on Smith Mountain Lake in Virginia. After about 10 minutes with their hooks in the water and no bites, they were all ready to give up. Marc said, "Fishing is a lot more fun if you catch fish."

Well, fishing was no fun at all for the disciples on the Sea of Galilee that night. In a way, that night of fishless fishing was a symbol of a deeper frustration. Their empty nets were a symbol of a deeper emptiness. Here was their dilemma: Jesus was alive and had appeared to them twice in Jerusalem, but when they went back home to Galilee, they did not know what to do next.

Many people today have a similar experience. They have a hard time connecting their religious experience with their everyday lives. We go to church, pray, read the Bible, and listen to sermons. Then we go back out into the real world, to the places where we work and live, and we have a hard time making connections between our religious beliefs and our daily lives.

Most of us know what it is like to spend all night fishing and not catch a thing. Most of us have pulled in our share of empty nets. We get up and go to work every day, but sometimes it just seems like we are going through the motions. Or we stay home, trying to keep the house in order and keep the kids clothed and fed and happy, and after a while we begin to wonder what's in it for me.

At one time or another for most of us, life becomes routine and ordinary and even frustrating. It's not that we are without hope. We know about the Resurrection. We know that the Jesus who died did not stay dead. But like the disciples, we have a hard time seeing what difference that makes for us in our everyday lives. Like the disciples, we have a hard time connecting that almost "too good to be true" message we hear on Sundays with the frustrations that come after Sunday has passed.

Then suddenly, without warning or expectation, a figure appeared on the distant shore. Just as day was breaking, just as the light was dawning, Jesus appeared on the beach and called out to those weary, hungry, frustrated, and disappointed disciples. "Have you caught any fish, boys?" "No, not a one." "Well, cast your net on the other side of the boat, and you will find some." Boy, was that an understatement! The disciples threw out their net on the right side and caught more fish than they had ever imagined. Someone in the group counted the fish: there were 153 big ones! All the disciples had done was to listen to Jesus, do what he said, and their net was filled.

At the risk of sounding idealistic and simplistic, so it is for us. When we listen to Jesus and do what he says, our nets are filled. Now, let me be clear about this. I'm not proclaiming some "health and wealth" gospel. I'm not saying that all you have to do is believe in Jesus and God will give you everything you ever wanted. No, faithfulness to Jesus does not guarantee a luxurious lifestyle. Believing in Jesus and doing what he says does not translate into a fatter bank account, a better job, a bigger house, and a new car. But listening to Jesus and doing what he says does have its rewards. When we allow the teachings of Christ to guide our lives, our nets will be filled. When we follow Jesus' instructions and cast our nets on the right side, we will catch more than we ever imagined. God will give us what we really need.

I read about a foreign missionary named Hazel Moon who died at the age of 73 in Appomattox, Virginia. I knew about another missionary from another era named Miss Moon, namely Lottie Moon. But this Miss Moon, Hazel, was a saint in her own right. For more than 34 years, Hazel was a missionary nurse to West Africa. She spent much of that time ministering to leprosy patients in Nigeria. She provided daily treatments for lepers in a camp near Ogbomosho. Not content just to provide medical treatment, she also managed a school and an adult literacy program for people with leprosy. Finally, she retired in 1981, and in 1982 Wake Forest University awarded Hazel Moon the honorary Doctor of Humanities degree. They presented her a citation that read:

> Whether creating special shoes and devices for those with deformities, or providing vocational training, or establishing villages for her patients' return to normal life, she brought faith and dignity, and long hours of work in late night and early morning to those from whom her love would not allow her to turn away.[1]

Hazel Moon never made a lot of money. She never married or had children. She never achieved fame, at least not by our standards. But in the Nigerian city of Ogbomosho, a church was made up of many of her former leprosy patients. They named it the Hazel Moon Baptist Church, because she cast her net on the right side of the boat, and the net always came up filled.

How then do we connect our religious experiences with our daily lives? How do we overcome the fatigue, frustrations, and disappointments that come to all of us from time to time? What do we do when we have been fishing all night and come up empty?

We listen to the voice of a figure on the distant shore. We can hear that voice saying: "Cast your net on the other side, my children. Try doing things my way for a while. Be kind to your neighbors. Love your enemies. Help those who are hurting. Do good to those who would hurt you. Serve others in Christ's name. Give to those in need. Forgive, and forgive, and forgive again. Cast your net on the right side, and you will be filled."

Breakfast can be more than just a meal to begin the day. Look at the disciples. That last breakfast with Jesus was a meal to begin the rest of their lives. It was a summons to a new way of living. It does not matter whether it is bread and fish cooked on a charcoal fire, or homemade biscuits and sugar syrup served on blue plates. When the breakfast is served with that much love, you remember it, and it changes you, and you learn to be loving too.

QUESTIONS FOR DISCUSSION/REFLECTION

1. Can you remember a time when you "fished" all night and caught nothing?
2. Has Jesus ever "fixed breakfast" for you?
3. What fish do you have to contribute to the meal?
4. What does this story say to you about following Jesus' instructions for your life?
5. What would a net full of fish look like in your circumstance?

NOTE

[1] *The Commission,* April 1989.

CHAPTER 12

DO YOU LOVE ME? FOLLOW ME
(John 21:15-19)

When they had finished breakfast, Jesus said to Simon Peter, "Simon, son of John, do you love me more than these?" He said to him, "Yes, Lord; you know that I love you." Jesus said to him, "Feed my lambs." (John 21:15 NRSV)

Three times Jesus asked Peter, "Do you love me?" and three times Peter said, "You know that I love you." Was Jesus hard of hearing, or was Peter not to be believed? After all, when Jesus had been arrested, Peter denied three times that he even knew Jesus (John 18:17, 25-27). If Peter really did love Jesus, then he would have to show it. He would show it by tending the flock of the Good Shepherd, and ultimately by laying down his life to glorify God. Although the Bible does not specify the manner of Peter's death, early church traditions say that he was martyred in Rome for following Jesus. Yes, Peter really did love Jesus. His denials were redeemed by a life of faith, witness, service, and love.

THE POWER OF WORDS
(John 21:15-19)

I don't know if you follow professional basketball. Even if you do not care anything about the NBA, you may remember hearing about the then-owner of the Los Angeles Clippers. In 2014 he made some racist comments to a girlfriend that were secretly recorded and then released to the media. The owner, worth an estimated $1.9 billion, told his girlfriend that he did not want her bringing any black men to see his team play basketball. Apparently, the owner thought that it reflected badly on him to have his girlfriend photographed with a black man while attending one of his basketball games. He also asked her to delete a photo she posted on Instagram of her and Magic Johnson. Those racist comments set off a firestorm of protest across the NBA and the sports world in general. Apparently, the owner had made racially offensive remarks before. In testimony from a court case, the owner defended trying to prevent blacks and Hispanics from renting apartments in a building he owned, because according to him, Hispanics were drunks and blacks smelled.

In reaction to the owner's comments, his team staged a silent protest before a playoff game. They took off their warm-up jackets and piled them in a heap in the center of the court. Underneath, they were wearing their team jerseys inside out, so that the Clippers logo was not showing. The players also wore black armbands and black socks as a sign of protest. Whether it was deliberate or not, the Clippers did not play well and lost that game by a wide margin.

Following the release of the recording of the team owner's racist comments, the commissioner of the NBA imposed the maximum fine and banished the Clippers' owner from all league and team activities. In a league where more than 75 percent of the players are African Americans, it is especially offensive for a team owner to utter racist comments. The owner was paying his players millions of dollars to play basketball, but actions do not always speak louder than words. Sometimes words speak louder than actions. Words have incredible power to hurt, but they also have the power to heal.

John 21 records how Jesus hurt Peter with his words, but then how Jesus healed Peter with his words. It was some time after the Resurrection, and the risen Jesus had appeared various times to those who loved him. In this incident some of the disciples had gone fishing on the Sea of Galilee. Simon Peter, Thomas, Nathanael, James, John, and others had gone out in a boat and fished all night. But they caught nothing.

Just after daybreak the risen Jesus appeared beside the sea, but they did not recognize it was Jesus. He called out to them and said, "You haven't caught any fish, have you?" "No," they replied. Jesus said, "Cast your net on the other side of the boat and you will catch some." So that's what they did. And soon the net was so full of fish that they could hardly haul it in. That was when John said to Peter, "It is the Lord!" Peter was so excited that he jumped into the water and swam ashore. The others followed in the boat, dragging the net full of fish behind them.

When the disciples reached the shore, they saw a charcoal fire burning, with fish and bread cooking on it. Jesus told them to bring some of the fish they had caught. Then he invited them to have breakfast. Jesus took the bread and gave it to them, and he did the same with the fish. This was now the third time that Jesus had appeared to his disciples after he was raised from the dead.

After breakfast Jesus had a heart-to-heart conversation with Peter. Three times Jesus asked Peter if he loved him. Peter was hurt by his words. If Jesus had asked Peter only once if he loved him, Peter might not have been so offended. But Jesus asked him again, and yet again. By the third time, Peter must have figured that Jesus did not believe him. Perhaps Jesus was remembering how Peter had denied him three times in the courtyard of the high priest on the night before Jesus was crucified. Maybe Jesus kept asking Peter, "Do you love me?" to remind Peter of what he had done. Peter had wept tears of regret that night, and his feelings of failure and remorse had probably been dogging him ever since. Now, this was like rubbing salt in the wound. But the hurtful words of Jesus became healing words.

Peter came to understand that Jesus was asking him, "Do you love me, do you love me, do you love me," not to hurt Peter, but to heal him. This was a new beginning. Peter had denied and failed Jesus three times, but Jesus was giving him another chance, not just to express his love for Jesus, but to demonstrate it. Both words and actions are necessary to tell the whole story.

Jesus said: "Feed my sheep." "Tend my lambs." "Follow me." Just telling Jesus that he loved him was not enough. Peter had to do something to show his love for Jesus.

"Lambs" and "sheep" were metaphors for the people Jesus was placing under Peter's pastoral care. Peter would demonstrate his love for Jesus by taking care of the people Jesus had entrusted to him. So, both words and actions are important.

Peter would go on to become a great leader in the early church, a preacher and a teacher, a healer and a role model. And in the end, Peter would give his life out of his devotion to Jesus. The scripture does not say exactly how it happened, but it implies that Peter would die a martyr's death. Early church tradition says that Peter was executed on orders of the Roman Emperor Nero, crucified, according to some writings, upside down. Peter, who three times denied his Lord, would glorify God through his death.

Words have the power both to hurt and to heal. This has never been truer than it is today. Our words can have far-reaching power. With social media, our words can reach out into cyberspace and go virtually anywhere. Careless comments on Facebook or Twitter or blogs can have unimagined consequences and cause much harm. With every smart phone a potential recording device, what we say and what we do can be preserved and replayed for unintended audiences.

When I was a pastor I had to be careful about what I said on Sunday mornings, because my sermons were recorded and posted on our church website. My words were not just for the people in the sanctuary. Anyone with a computer could listen to what I said. I know of people in other states who would listen to my sermons on a regular basis through the podcasts.

Jesus was aware that our words have great power. Words are like a window into the soul. In Matthew 12 Jesus said, "For out of the abundance of the heart the mouth speaks." Jesus went on to say, "I tell you, on the day of judgment you will have to give an account for every careless word you utter, for by your words you will be justified, and by your words you will be condemned" (vv. 34b, 36-37). So, there is great power in words. Some words can hurt, but other words can help and heal.

As a pastor, sometimes I wondered about my words. I wondered if what I said really made a difference in anyone's life. People were always coming and going, and sometimes I wondered if what I said mattered. But every so often someone would say something that made me realize my efforts were not in vain.

When a young woman in our congregation, Katie Smith, got married, three young ladies who had been raised in our church served as Katie's matrons of honor. At the wedding reception the three gave a speech directed at the bride. The young women were Katie's two sisters, Becky and Jennie, and her best friend, Lessa. In their remarks to Katie, they talked about how they had all grown up together in the church. They talked about how they had all dreamed of getting married, and they even mentioned some of the young men in the youth group they dreamed of marrying. It turned out that all of them found other husbands, not the young men from our church. But it was obvious from their remarks that the church was an important part of their lives. They even mentioned some older married couples in the church who were role models for them.

Hearing what Becky, Jennie, and Lessa had to say made me feel good. I've known Lessa and the Smith sisters since they were little girls. I watched them grow up. I baptized all four of them. I officiated at all four of their weddings. They are almost like daughters to Linda and me. To hear them express appreciation for their church family almost made me cry. Words have great power to hurt, but words also have power to help and to heal. The words we speak can have a tremendous impact on others' lives.

In the fullness of time God spoke his Word to us. John said, "the Word became flesh and lived among us, and we have seen his glory, the glory as of a father's only son, full of grace and truth" (John 1:14). The Word becoming flesh was Jesus. God spoke that Word, not to hurt but to heal, not to destroy but to save, not to condemn but to give life. When Jesus died on the cross, his death spoke volumes about how much God loves us. And when God raised Jesus from the dead, God demonstrated that he always has the last Word. Nothing can separate us from the love of Christ. What more do we need to say?

THE SECRET TO CONTENTMENT
(John 21:15-17)

Who is more content: a woman with seven children or a woman with $7 million? Answer: the woman with seven children, because she does not want any more. Ah, contentment… More than money, more than even children, contentment is what we want out of life. But how do we find true contentment?

Simon Peter was not content the morning of the last breakfast. In fact, he was very discontented with his life. We can understand why. Jesus had come back from the dead. He had been raised from the grave. He was once again alive and with his disciples. You would think that Peter would have been excited about that, and he was—for a while. But soon Peter's elation gave way to guilt. He could hardly look Jesus in the eye. After Jesus had been arrested, Peter was asked three times if he were one of Jesus' followers. And three times Peter denied it. Afterwards, Peter was so ashamed of his cowardice that he went out and wept bitterly. But he never got the chance to speak to Jesus about it until that moment beside the Sea of Galilee.

The disciples had been fishing all night, but at daybreak they spied a figure on the shore. It was Jesus, risen from the dead. Jesus prepared breakfast, and after they had eaten, Jesus and Peter walked away from the others for a heartfelt chat. Jesus wanted to know if Peter really loved him, after what Peter had done. It was an important question. Peter's betrayal was like a wall between them. They could not be close again until something was done to tear down that wall. Jesus needed to know if Peter were genuinely sorry for what he had done. And Peter needed the opportunity to profess his love for Jesus and to receive forgiveness.

So, three times Jesus asked him, "Peter, do you love me?" It was once for each denial. "Yes, Lord, you know I love you," Peter answered, each time with more anguish, more remorse. Jesus was not trying to make Peter feel worse. Peter probably could not feel worse than he already felt. He had been hating himself ever since that terrible night. But the only way for Peter to get past his guilt was to face it squarely. Then the healing could begin.

I don't know about you, but I have a guilty conscience when I do something wrong. If I hurt someone by something I have done, or if I say a careless or unkind word, or if I fail to do what I know is right, I generally feel terrible about it. Sometimes I can go to the person I have hurt and apologize. Other times, all I can do is ask God to forgive me. Either way, I've got to do something to deal with my guilt and try to set things right.

Guilt that is not dealt with can eat away at our souls. I know some people who feel guilty about a mistake they made years ago. Instead of confessing their sin and receiving forgiveness, they keep circling around and coming back to it, like a comet caught in an orbit. Judas was like that. He could not deal with his guilt after he betrayed Jesus. So, he ended up killing himself. Peter, to his credit, took a better way. After the Resurrection, he went back to Jesus and dared believe that Jesus would accept him and forgive him. Peter knew that was the only way he could ever be happy again.

There are many obstacles that can stand in the way of our contentment, but surely one of the greatest obstacles to peace of mind is unresolved guilt. That was one of the reasons we had a big cross erected in the Village Baptist Church sanctuary all day on Good Friday. It was an opportunity for people to sit and pray, and if they wished, to leave some burden at the cross. At the end of the evening, around 10:00 p.m., I went into the sanctuary and removed slips of paper that people had stuck on the cross. I did not read any of them. I took them home and threw them into the fireplace and burned them. Maybe some of those slips of paper contained a confession, or a request for forgiveness. If they did, my burning them was symbolic of forgiveness, for that was what the sacrifice of Jesus on the cross was all about.

Jesus died on the cross to forgive us of our sins. But sometimes we have a hard time accepting that forgiveness. Sometimes we have a hard time accepting ourselves. That's where I find this story of Jesus and Peter helpful. Jesus did more than forgive Peter. Jesus gave Peter something meaningful to do. It was more than doing some act of penance. Jesus was giving Peter a whole new way of life. From that day on, Peter was to be about feeding sheep. Of course, Jesus was speaking metaphorically. He was talking about people who needed Peter's help and care. Peter could feed Jesus' sheep by serving others. This was the way out for Peter, the way out of his guilt, the way out of his self-loathing, the way out of his discontent. By giving himself in service to others, Peter would discover the joy of his salvation.

The 19th-century German poet Goethe wrote a dramatic poem, "Faust," about a man who sold his soul to the devil. In medieval legends on which the character was based, the philosopher Faust sells his soul to the devil in exchange for knowledge or power. In Goethe's version, Faust sells his soul for just one moment of contentment. Faust wants a moment so fulfilling that he could say, "Let this moment linger, it is so good." The devil proceeds to give Faust everything he desires. Faust is given wealth, power, women, status. But because Faust is a selfish man, it does not satisfy. He accumulates more and more, but he still feels empty inside. Near the end of his life, however, Faust gets involved in helping to build dikes for some poor farmers. It is hard, back-breaking work, but strangely fulfilling. Only then is Faust able to say, for the first time, "Let this moment linger, it is so good." Faust finally discovers that the secret to contentment is not gaining more and more, but in giving of yourself. When Jesus told Peter to feed his sheep, he was telling Peter that the secret to contentment is to give one's self in service to others.

In his book, *Modern Man in Search of a Soul*, psychiatrist Carl Jung wrote, "About a third of my patients are suffering from no clinically definable neurosis, but from the emptiness of their lives." Jung frequently told those patients that if they wanted to feel better about themselves, they needed to go out and find someone to help.

George Müller was born in 1805 in Germany, the son of a Prussian tax collector. Although he was raised in the state-sponsored Lutheran Church, Müller was anything but a Christian as a youth. He spent his allowances on drinking and gambling, and when his own money ran out, he stole from his father's tax collections. When he was 14, his mother died unexpectedly. Not even aware she was ill, young Müller was out playing cards past midnight on Saturday, and then he skipped church on Sunday to go out drinking. His father had to track him down to drag him to his mother's funeral. You might think that such an experience would have changed him, but at the age of 16 Müller was arrested for failing to pay numerous hotel bills. He spent three weeks in jail before his father paid his debts and bailed him out.

At the age of 19, at his father's insistence, Müller was sent to the university to study for the Lutheran ministry. As you might have guessed, his heart was not in it. Müller continued his drinking and wild lifestyle along with many of his classmates. He estimated that out of 900 divinity students, only nine had any thoughts about God. At the age of 20, however, something happened to Müller that had a profound effect upon his life.

He was invited to go to a prayer meeting instead of going out drinking, and for some reason he went. Something happened at that prayer meeting that began to fill the emptiness in Müller's life. Later he wrote, "I was happy; though if I had been asked why I was happy, I could not have explained it." Müller concluded that God had begun to work in his life.

Within a few months, he moved to England to begin study to become a missionary. There in London he became associated with a small group of believers and became their pastor.

While living in London, Müller became aware of the many orphans who were living on the streets. Epidemics would sweep through the city, sometimes killing the parents, leaving their children alone. Orphaned children were consigned to "workhouses," which were little more than slave labor factories. Their food, clothing, and lodging were horrendous, and they were forced to work long hours for no pay, with harsh discipline. Many orphaned children ran away from the workhouses and lived on the streets. Many young girls were forced into prostitution, and young boys took up thievery. Müller was shocked by these circumstances and set out to provide a better alternative.

He acquired a remodeled house and took in 30 orphaned girls. Eventually his work expanded to include five large houses, dormitories really, caring for 2,000 orphans at a time. Müller devoted the rest of his life to caring for orphans and distributing Bibles and religious tracts. In his early years, George Müller had lived a life of which he had much to be ashamed. But God began to work in his life, and Müller came to recognize that his life could be redeemed in service to others.[1]

Instead of wallowing in guilt, Müller set about to serve others in Christ's name. More than 10,000 orphans were saved from the streets of London because George

Müller (1805–1898) did something about his guilt. He demonstrated his love for Jesus by feeding his sheep. As Christians, we serve others in Christ's name, not out of guilt, but out of gratitude. God has forgiven us through the sacrifice of his Son, and we demonstrate our love for Jesus when we feed his sheep.

FEED MY SHEEP
(John 21:15-17)

The book, *In Retrospect* by Robert McNamara, is part analysis, part confession, of what went wrong during the Vietnam War. McNamara served as Secretary of Defense in the Kennedy and Johnson administrations during the escalation of the war. His book stirred up a whole new debate about that tragic time in our nation's history. It also intensified feelings of betrayal among many veterans who served our nation in Vietnam.

In the book McNamara admitted he knew the war was unwinnable as early as 1967. He wrote, "we totally underestimated the nationalistic aspect of Ho Chi Minh's movement." The United States saw it as a war against communism. The North Vietnamese and Viet Cong saw it as a war of national survival. Because President Johnson feared an all-out war would bring China and the Soviet Union into the conflict, the United States tried to wage a limited war. That strategy was doomed to failure. In the fall of 1967, McNamara told President Johnson that "we could not achieve our objective in Vietnam through any reasonable military means."[2] The Joint Chiefs of Staff, however, and some influential members of Congress, took a more optimistic view. McNamara was removed as Secretary of Defense and made president of the World Bank in 1968.

Many veterans still feel a deep sense of betrayal because McNamara did not push harder for a diplomatic solution after he concluded the war could not be won through military means. They blame McNamara for sending them into a futile conflict, and for the deaths of so many of their comrades. Vietnam was a bitter experience for our country, but perhaps McNamara's memoir was a necessary step in the recovery process. As the ancient Greek dramatist Aeschylus wrote, "The reward of suffering is experience."

Betrayal is one of the worst emotions a person can feel. Betrayal may be even worse than the hurt that comes from losing a loved one. To be sure, death brings its own kind of pain, but in most cases, that pain is not intentional. In the case of betrayal, the hurt could have been avoided. Betrayal means disloyalty; it means a breach of trust. There is hardly anything worse than having someone whom you trusted stab you in the back. That is the way many Vietnam veterans feel. They feel that their government was disloyal to them, and in effect, stabbed them in the back by sending them into a war we knew we could not win. It is hard not to feel bitter when you feel betrayed.

That is why this story in our scripture passage is so remarkable. Peter had betrayed Jesus, not just once, but three times in the courtyard of the high priest. While Jesus was on trial, while his life hung in the balance, three times Peter had a chance to stand up for Jesus, but three times Peter let him down. According to Luke's Gospel, after the third denial Jesus turned and looked at Peter across the courtyard (22:61-62). It must have been a look that seared Peter's soul. No wonder Peter went out and wept bitterly after that. Is there anything worse than to betray a friend?

So, this encounter beside the Sea of Tiberias was all the more remarkable. It was after the Resurrection, and Peter and the other disciples were back home in Galilee. They had been fishing all night when Jesus appeared to them on the shore at daybreak. After fixing breakfast for them, Jesus took Peter aside. It's a wonder Peter could even look Jesus in the eye after what he had done. Peter had stabbed Jesus in the back with his three denials, and Jesus knew it, and Peter knew that Jesus knew it. Now Jesus asked Peter, "do you really love me?" not once, but three times. It was not that Jesus was being vindictive or trying to make Peter feel guilty for his disloyalty. Peter already felt guilty. He had been bearing a huge burden of guilt ever since he heard the rooster crow that morning of the Crucifixion. No, Jesus confronted Peter not to punish him, but to enable the recovery process to begin.

If you live long enough, you probably are going to find yourself on both sides of the betrayal equation. You probably are going to feel betrayed at some point in your life, and you probably are going to say something or do something that causes someone else to feel hurt. When betrayal happens, there is only one way to get over it, and that is to deal with it. We cannot ignore it or try to forget about it or pretend it did not happen. The only way to heal a broken relationship is to talk about it with the person involved.

Of course, it was terribly painful for Peter to talk about the betrayal with Jesus. Peter was in agony because Jesus kept asking him, "Do you love me? Do you love me? Do you love me?" But that was the only way Peter and Jesus could get over that breach in their relationship. Peter had betrayed Jesus. That was done. No words could change what had happened. But while they could not change the past, they could change the future. There could be a new beginning in their relationship. There could be a new understanding that would allow them to put the past behind them and start to trust each other again. There could be forgiveness and reconciliation. And that is precisely what took place.

When Jesus said to Peter, "feed my sheep," he was saying in effect: "Peter, I trust you again. I trust you enough that I am asking you to take care of the sheep in my flock." Of course, Jesus was using a metaphor. Jesus was not a literal shepherd of animals; he was talking about his followers as his sheep. And Jesus was asking Peter to look after them.

This may be the origin of the tradition that made Peter the first pastor of the early church. That is what a pastor is, a shepherd, one who looks after the flock. But I think we miss the point if we think that this command applied only to Peter. God calls some persons to be pastors of the flock, but he calls all Christians to care for one another. All the followers of Jesus are to look out for each other. Caring for the flock is not only the pastor's job, or the deacons' job, or the job of the church staff. Jesus calls all of us to be caregivers. If Jesus could take a miserable failure like Peter and trust him to care for the flock, Jesus can use each of us too.

There are many ways we can care for one another. We can greet each other warmly in church services and let worshippers around us know that we are glad to see them. We can seek out newcomers and strangers in our midst and make them feel welcome. We can be on the lookout for persons who are on the fringes, those who might be left out unless we take the initiative to include them. We can volunteer to participate in church and community organizations, programs, projects, and ministries. We serve Christ by feeding his sheep.

Betrayal is a terrible experience, but there is one thing that is more powerful than betrayal, and that is love. Knowing that I am loved enables me to love others. Jesus loves every one of us. If we love him, we show him: We feed his sheep.

QUESTIONS FOR DISCUSSION/REFLECTION

1. Why do you think Jesus wanted to talk with Simon Peter after breakfast?
2. Have you ever done something that you needed to talk with Jesus about?
3. Who are the sheep/lambs that Jesus was talking about?
4. What are some ways that we can feed or tend Jesus' sheep/lambs?
5. What was Jesus predicting when he told Peter that he would stretch out his hands and someone would fasten a belt around him and take him where he did not wish to go?

NOTES

[1] *Christian History Newsletter*, Winter 1997.
[2] *Newsweek*, April 17, 1995.

About the Author

Bruce Salmon served for 33 years as pastor of Village Baptist Church in Bowie, Maryland. During that time, he preached almost 1,500 original Sunday morning sermons, including more than 80 sermons on the resurrection stories in Matthew, Mark, Luke, and John. For the last 18 years of his ministry, he taught a Sunday morning pastor's class in which adults read and discussed entire books of the Bible. He also led winter, summer, and Lenten Sunday evening adult studies that covered various topics and Bible books, including the following:

- Introducing the New Testament
- The Sermon on the Mount
- The Life of Christ
- The Life of Paul
- The Passion of Jesus
- The Jesus of the Bible
- Genesis
- Exodus
- Joshua
- 1 Samuel
- 2 Samuel
- Isaiah
- Ezekiel
- Malachi
- Matthew
- Mark
- Luke
- John
- Acts
- Romans
- 2 Corinthians
- Hebrews
- James
- Revelation

A native of Fort Worth, Texas, Salmon received the Bachelor of Arts degree with a major in English from Baylor University and the Master of Divinity and Doctor of Ministry degrees from the Southern Baptist Theological Seminary. He also received the Master of Arts in Counseling Psychology from Bowie State University, with a specialization in Clinical Pastoral Counseling.

Salmon has served on several committees of the D.C. Baptist Convention and on several commissions of the Baptist World Alliance. In addition to this volume and others in the series *Spelunking Scripture*,* he is the author of *Storytelling in Preaching* (BSSB, 1988) and *Preaching for the Long Haul: A Case Study on Long-Term Pastoral Ministry* (Nurturing Faith, 2019).

Salmon is husband to wife Linda, father to grown children Amy and Marc, father-in-law to Stacey, and grandfather to granddaughter Ford. In addition to studying the Bible, his interests include spectator sports, current events, music, museums, golf, and travel.

*For more information and blogs, visit www.spelunkingscripture.com.

www.ingramcontent.com/pod-product-compliance
Lightning Source LLC
Chambersburg PA
CBHW071006160426
43193CB00012B/1943